To —
My friend
Susan a Bride
magnificent Love
Light of our
Bridle

WHO DO YOU THINK YOU ARE ?

BRIAN D. JONES

iUniverse®

WHO DO YOU THINK YOU ARE?

iUniverse books may be ordered through booksellers or by contacting:

iUniverse
1663 Liberty Drive
Bloomington, IN 47403
www.iuniverse.com
1-800-Authors (1-800-288-4677)

ISBN: 978-1-5320-7663-3 (sc)
ISBN: 978-1-5320-7662-6 (e)

Library of Congress Control Number: 2019908034

Print information available on the last page.

iUniverse rev. date: 07/20/2019

Contents

Acknowledgments

I gratefully acknowledge the writings of many spiritual teachers, including Dr. Deepak Chopra, Dr. Wayne Dyer, Gregg Braden, Marianne Williamson, Neale Donald Walsch, Gary Renard, Gary Zukav, Edgar Cayce, Tina Louise Spalding, Tom and Linda Carpenter, Robert Holden, and Barry and Joyce Vissell.

I would also like to thank all the various members of *A Course in Miracles* groups I have attended, as well as those of other spiritual study groups I have been a part of. A special thank-you to Scott Wilcox, who has been instrumental in getting all these writings ready for publication.

Dedication

I dedicate this book of inspired writings to my teachers, Jesus (author of *A Course in Miracles* and *Jesus—My Autobiography*), and Bill Wilson and Dr. Bob Smith (cofounders of Alcoholics Anonymous).

Their teachings have been passed down to me lovingly by too many persons to mention here.

Preface

This is primarily a book of poetry, but I decided to include several experiences I have had, such as a song that I dreamed and several inspired writings I received during meditation. I have also included several other songs that just came to me by way of some inspiration. I don't sit around writing poetry. In fact, I have no training in writing and have never written anything before this.

All of these experiences and compositions have spoken to me and are indicative of where I was on my journey at the time I wrote them. But I find that when I share them with others, they often speak to them as well.

All I ever wanted from life was to love and be loved. So, a few of these writings deal with love. Several of them deal with my recovery from alcoholism through a twelve-step program. Some of them use lines or ideas taken from a twelve-step book. Many of them deal with the teaching of *A Course in Miracles*, and you can also find lines and ideas taken from that book.

The poem titled "Recovery Still Spoken Here" lists many people and what they actually said. I have taken a small amount of liberty in this poem in order to maintain the rhyme scheme. But each one of the people mentioned literally said what is recorded or put forth the ideas set down in this poem.

In my meditation writings, I address my questions to Jesus, whom I refer to as J.

The cover photo of a sunrise is meant to symbolize the light that is coming on inside me and throughout the world at this time.

When I reread these poems, they again speak to me, just as they did to begin with. I hope the ideas expressed here speak to you as well.

A Dream

I went to a party at a friend's house with another friend, Barry. Upon leaving the party, Barry was seated in the front passenger seat of my car. As we went up the hill from the house, we encountered a large pile of sticks and branches in the middle of the road. I got out of the car and cleared them out of the way. I returned to the car and again started up the hill. I looked over at Barry and saw that he was no longer there. The hooded figure of death was sitting in his seat.

I continued up the hill and came to the main road. When I applied the brakes, there were none. We continued onto the road and drove directly into oncoming headlights. I felt myself rise up out of my bed as if I were a balloon. I gently bounced off the cathedral ceiling in my bedroom, and I heard myself say, "Is that all there is?"

I woke up, and the fear of death left me at that point.

A Meditation

During a meditation, I saw a heavy wooden door with a rounded top. It appeared to be a door to a medieval church. On the front of this door there was a wooden peg with a heavy iron key ring hanging from it. On this ring, there were several iron keys.

I saw a hand take the key ring from the door and offer the keys to me. A voiceless voice said to me, "These are the keys to the kingdom." I replied, "But I don't deserve them."

I then saw a highway bridge, the kind with a green metal superstructure above the roadway. There was an extra superstructure lying on top of the regular one. A large hand removed it and held it upside down under the bridge. I saw a large thumb shooting sparks at it as if welding it in place. The voice then said to me, "I will build you a better foundation."

As I look back at the past thirty to thirty-five years, I can clearly see that this is what has happened and is still happening. I have been led to one book after another, one teaching after another, all leading me in one direction. They have all had a positive impact on me.

Warriors of Love

In the mid-1990s as I was getting into my hot tub one night, the voiceless voice said to me, "We are the warriors of love." When I questioned that statement, the voice continued:

"Warriors need not be engaged in physical onslaught. Rather, they are the protectors of hallowed ground, not easily won."

Today I see that sobriety and spiritual growth, as well as the opening of my heart, is the hallowed ground. And it certainly was not easily won. I need to maintain all three of these.

The Man I Was

Here's to the man I was, the one who shed the tears,
the one who lived with resentments, anger, and fears.

It was he who survived the tough times, the storms, and
the rain.
It was he who suffered through frustration, loneliness,
and pain.

Here's to the man who kept on without any hope.
Here's to the man who continued to the end of his rope.

It was he, a good man who only wanted to love,
who, in a moment of despair, cried out to the One above:

"God, if there is one, please help me now!
I'm so tired of living without knowing how."

"You can't on your own, try though you may, son.
I will build you a better foundation."

He then spoke to me through many others.
He spoke through my sisters and through my brothers.

Clear away the wreckage of your past.
We'll help you build something that will last.

Admit your faults to Him and to your fellows,
and He will hold your rage from now until it mellows.

Managing your life is the great delusion.
Follow us, they said, for we have found the solution.

Choose again, now, to stop chasing your every whim.
Give yourself to God *as you understand Him.*

Let *Him* guide your life, not your fathers and your mothers.
Great events will come to pass for you and countless
others.

So here's to the man I honor now who lived so long ago.
His memories are mine; the rest is just a glow.

Keep Coming Back

The loss of my children, my home, and my wife
left me unable to cope with my life.

Filled with resentment, anger, and fear,
I turned to dark bars, whiskey, and beer.

Loneliness was my constant friend.
It seemed as though it never would end.

And try as I might, I just couldn't see
why everything negative happened to me.

I cried and I cried, writhing in pain,
with a knot in my stomach and nothing to gain.

Why did so many treat me so bad?
Everyone else seemed happy and glad.

I cried out to God, whom I did not know,
"If there is help for me, please make it so."

My plea was soon answered. New friends took me round
and went to great lengths to share what they'd found.

They were all friendly. They approached me with
greetings.

6

"Read the Big Book, and go to these meetings."

A new way of living, now free of drink,
had saved all their lives, brought them back from the brink.

They said it was simple, just follow their lead.
Take these twelve steps, and you'll get what you need.

And now I am one of them, back from the brink,
with a new way of living, a new way to think.

Free of resentment, anger, and fear,
free of dark bars, whiskey, and beer.

I now tell others, "If you want to quit drinking,
clean up your past. Find a *new* way of thinking.

Leave your old haunts. Pull away from the pack.
Stick with the winners—and keep coming back!"

Recovery Still Spoken Here

As I strolled through a strange town one night,
through a church basement door came a strange, eerie
light.

As I pushed open the door,
I saw a familiar sight,

tables and chairs
to the left and the right.

Someone said, "Brian, how do you feel?"
I turned, and I spotted Dennis O'Neill.

I saw Grant Hill with his bald little head.
"Sit down, shut up, and listen," he said.

Gil stood and pointed at me with a sneer.
"I've been wondering when *you* were going to get here."

And there was Big Bob, larger than life,
seated next to Karlynn, his cute little wife.

"Religion is the politics of spirituality," she said.
And I began to nod my head.

Corky and Bill were both in there, eh?
These two Canadians have something to say!

Corky muttered, "You can't get here from where I was."
Many heads nodded, and I heard a faint buzz.

"Ask 'What do I need today?' whenever you feel a lack."
When Bill C. said that, I was taken aback.

Then Ron M. rose with a sigh.
"You people taught me how to love," said he with a tear
in his eye.

"AA to the rescue," Adrienne said.
And a cavalry bugle went off in my head.

"God loves me enough to bring me this far, but He loves
me too much to leave me here,"
uttered Marge Quinn, with a smile and a tear.

Then Will C. began to share.
As he rambled on, I nearly dozed off in my chair.

What does he mean? What is he saying?
Something about God, meditation, and praying.

With one last sentence, it all became clear.
What he said is what *I* needed to hear.

This room's not ornate. It's nothing real fancy.
Hey, here comes Marilyn, Val, Delores, Sandy, Rosie, and
Nancy.

Next is Russ without any sleeve:
"We're not cured. We have a daily reprieve."

Then Nancy: "These kids are not ours; they're only on loan.
Our job is to love them and give them a home."

And Rosie: "Thanks for giving me something to chew on.
For it's me who needs to hear what I just advised you on."

Then said I (well, someone should give it),
"The spiritual life is not a theory. *We have to live it.*"

Jim D. then stood up.
"Love never filled *my* little cup.

After my parents' abrupt removal,
I've spent my whole life seeking love and approval.

But love is not something we must get to live.
Love is the one thing we really must give."

At this I bent over, flooded with tears.
Their fingerprints had been on my heart for all those years.

As my eyes then flitted to all of the tables,
I saw many more chairs with names on their labels.

Judith and Lester, John, Jerry, and Delle,
I knew all of them very well.

Randy, Patrick, Denny, and Don. Bill D., Jeff P., both Steves, and Jerome.

One thing was clear: we all felt at home.

There was Paul, Chris, Martha Ann, Jim Robbins, and Pete.
They all filed in and took their seats.

Scott, Ralph, Mike, Rich, Brad, Barney, Jim Murphy, and Dave.
I looked over at them and gave a slight wave.

'Hey," said Dave, "save one of those chairs.
We need to have room for the Ol' Man Upstairs!"

The last to come in was old Denny Scuch.
Never to so many have I owed so much.

By the time they got around to passing the basket,
I remembered Big Bob, who passed away in Tonasket.

Once more I glanced from chair to chair.
Dr. Bob and Bill Wilson, they were both there.

And who is chairing this meeting in the heavens?
My God, it's my late sponsor George Evans.

"How's this working for you?" he cried.
In that moment, I knew that I'd died.

And then it all became so very clear.
Recovery was *still* being spoken up here.

This Special Room

We gather each week within this special room
to discuss the ego's world of impending doom,

to learn how to step aside and avoid the train coming
down the track,
to finally let go of all our guilt and our attack,

to reach out with trust and with gentle ease,
and to grasp the Spirit's part of the trapeze.

And if we should fail in our attempt at it to get,
we can rest assured that we have a safety net.

For if we pay attention, we will find
that all it really takes is to have a change of mind.

And who would continue walking down the track,
hearing only the ego's voice say, "Clickety-clack,
clickety-clack"?

We can sense the Holy Spirit's sweet perfume
as soon as we come through the door of this special,
special room.

Building the Arch

We are building an arch through which we shall walk
free people at last,
through which we shall walk when all our tests we have
passed,

when all of our judgments we have let go,
when we have learned to live in the flow,

when we've chosen to live in a state of trust,
when we've allowed the ego to be crushed,

when with conflict we've had enough,
when we've opted to live in a state of love,

when we've chosen to walk the high road,
when we've chosen love and tolerance as our code,

when we've recalled that we're not divided—
and with this remembrance we are delighted.

It's only then that we are at last free,
free to be who we are meant to be.

My Purpose

My purpose in this world of strife
is to awaken to the Spirit and let Him run my life,

to operate in a new and different mode
where love and tolerance have become my code,

to turn in all things to the Father of Light,
and to finally end this lifelong fight.

For to cease fighting everything and everyone
is to finally let the Spirit's will be done,

to let sanity return
to where anger and judgment churn,

to finally give up on the delusion
that I can find happiness in an illusion,

to stop burning energy in this hell
by trying to arrange life to suit me well,

to open the door to this self-constructed cage
and finally exit from this stage,

to stop playing this endless role
and return home, where I am whole.

Denny's Strange Odyssey

On his way to work, he came to the light.
Work to the left, liquor store to the right.

Damn car veered to the right.
It always did when it came to that light.

"Give me a half pint," he said to the clerk.
"It'll be enough to get me to work.

Or maybe a pint, just to get me through the day,
of the stuff that's pushing my daughter away.

Say, make it a fifth—it'll be all right—
of the stuff that makes my wife cry all night.

Or better yet, make it a half gallon, pal.
She'll understand; she's a good old gal."

Thus, went a day in the odyssey of Denny.
It wasn't unique; God knows there were many.

And if *we* should say "It could never happen to me,"
we need only ask Denny of *his* strange odyssey.

Adrienne

"Oh, Lordy, I was mean,"
said the kindly old woman named Adrienne.

"People coming would cross the street,"
said this little old woman so sweet.

"AA to the rescue," she cried.
And something began to change inside.

Grant shouted, "Sit down, shut up, and listen,"
she recalled, and her eyes began to glisten.

She then recounted her miraculous story
of her journey from hate to love's sweet glory.

And now anyone would be happy to meet
Adrienne, this little old woman so sweet.

Meditation Writing I

I ask, "J, what would You say to me today?" His reply is as follows:

Greetings, My brother. To know that I am the Way means that in order to rise up to where I am, you need to follow the path I have laid out for you. It is the path to life, not death. To know that I am the light means that you must let Me shine My light on this path so that you might see it more clearly.

Hence, I am the Way. Follow Me. I am the light; let Me show you the way. I am the life—this is the way to eternal life. I am the truth; I will not lie to you, My brother. But beware the path of separation. It is the path of darkness, lies, and death. That is all.

Love,

J

Meditation Writing II

I ask, "J, what would You say to me today?" His reply is as follows:

Greetings, My brother. All is one! This is all you need to know. There is no separation, only the appearance of it in your dream. Upon awakening from a dream, do you ever say, "That was so real"? It seemed to be real, but it was not. That is what you will say upon awakening from your present nightmare: "That seemed so real. Thank God it was not!"

Dreams are meant to show you the way back home. And this one is no different. This dream is showing you that you are not at home. How could you be at home in a place where everything is so threatening? Home is supposed to be a place of safe harbor where one is shielded from the storms of life. This place where you currently seem to be is not a place of safe harbor. You are caught up in the middle of a raging tornado.

Choose to follow Me, and I will lead you out of it. Choose to follow your ego (belief in separation), and you will bounce from one storm to the next with little rest in between. Come home! Find peace with Me, My brother. That is all.

Love,

J

Abandonment

What my mother taught me from my birth
was that I was no good, that I had no worth.

And I soaked this up when, as a child,
my consciousness became defiled.

It wasn't true, but I was filled with terror
at the prospect of abandonment, a fundamental error.

How could I be abandoned by the One
whose presence in me is never done?

And now I have been led to discover
that I have attracted to myself a substitute mother,

someone new to take over Mom's role
and unknowingly work to fulfill her goal,

someone who can remind me to feel rejected,
to feel all alone and quite disconnected.

But the fact is that she is not at fault.
It's my belief that it's true that I must halt.

For according to my belief, so shall it be done unto me.
And I must let go of it if I wish ever to be free.

Choose Once More

In my mind is where my problems began,
when I chose to follow the ego's dark plan.

The ego's ploy is to keep me aligned
with my belief in separateness always in mind.

But my salvation comes only from me,
not from anything outside that I see.

I must turn in all things to the Father of Light
and leave behind the ego's dark world of fright.

All I need do is to choose once more
and follow Spirit through heaven's bright door.

I must change my mind and see only one
in order for Spirit's plan to be done.

Cobwebs of the Mind

As I search through the attic up the stair,
I see cobwebs hanging everywhere.

Bony skeletons of days long past up here
amid feelings of shame, guilt, and fear.

Vampire bats hang from every stud,
baring their teeth, screaming for my blood.

Why go on and on reviewing the days of my life?
Why continue to relive those times of tears and strife?

Why not choose to live in this moment, this time
called now?
What sort of treasure could be hidden among cobwebs
anyhow?

Focus

We are all one with God and with each other,
connected by Him to our sister and brother.

But the ego says I'm separate, apart from the whole.
This faulty belief may take its toll.

For even mistaken beliefs have power
to cause an illness to grow and to flower,

to bring on depression, resentment, and need,
to cause these things to mate and to breed.

For as a man thinketh, so is he.
According to his beliefs, so shall he be.

Whatever I focus my thoughts on will grow.
And then it becomes my friend or my foe.

When I think about kindness, love, and forgiving,
it brings to my life a better way of living.

But if I focus on enemies and foes,
it brings into my life depression and woes.

So, I choose to think these things: love and compassion.
On this solid foundation, a new life will be fashioned.

I Am Not a Victim

I am not a victim of the world I see.
Whenever I'm upset, there's something wrong with me.

And a good measure of the amount of guilt I hold within
is the result of how many times I behold my brother's sin.

And what I see in my brothers, I also see in me.
In truth there are no others. This is the golden key.

I need only change my thoughts to change what I believe.
For this mad world is built on what it is that I perceive.

The Way We Live

We've been taught, so we already know,
that what we reap is what we sow.

Our thoughts and our words, that's what we plant.
So why *do* we condemn, rage, boast, and rant?

Why do we insist on remaining apart?
Let us now plant love and acceptance in our hearts.

Love and acceptance, they're the same things.
Let us practice them now and see what it brings.

Must we continue to blame, to gripe, and to grumble?
Let us now make the choice to be meek and be humble.

For it's not about what we preach;
the way we live is what we teach.

And who learns what we teach?
It's us, not them, whom we reach.

This Belief Must Be Undone

I came here and then I found
a world turned upside down,

a world turned topsy-turvy,
a world where nothing is sturdy,

a world where love has been replaced with blame,
a world where we are filled with fear, guilt and shame,

a world gone mad with its plans and schemes,
where absolutely nothing is as it seems,

where division and hatred seem to prevail,
where millions starve or are put in jail,

where our leaders accuse each other of lying,
where vast numbers of us seem to be dying.

We must undo this mad idea of being apart.
We must feel and express the love in our hearts.

We must remember that we are all one.
This insane belief in separation must be undone.

Ain't It Awful?

Let's talk about everything that's wrong.
"Ain't it awful?" It's the nature of our song.

Let's sing out the lyrics loud and strong:
"Ain't it awful?" It's the title of our song.

From the weather to politics, we ramble on and on,
unaware that more problems are what we spawn.

For the universe will correspond to the nature of our song.
"Ain't it awful?" we all sing in unison as we go along.

But what if we were to alter the nature of our song?
We'd soon have little to talk about with the throng.

What if we choose now to sing out, "Ain't it great?"
It's clear that we'd soon have no one else to hate.

From our previous position in life we'd waffle,
and we'd loosen our ties to "Ain't it awful?"

"Ain't it awful?" would be replaced,
and gratitude would be embraced.

So, let's all sing out now, let's sing out loud and clear.
"Ain't it awful?" is what we no longer wish to hear.

The World of Spirit

Ah, what fools these mortals be
who believe only what the human eye can see,

never knowing that the world of form is created by their thought
and that the world of form is where all their battles are continuously fought.

But the world of Spirit floats above the battleground.
The world of Spirit is where true reality is found.

And the world of form, which seems to be upon us crushing,
is in truth much ado about nothing.

I Am Not the Thinker

I am not the thinker of these thoughts, I think I think.
From this great truth I must not shrink.

I have become a strong believer
in the idea that my mind is but a receiver.

And when I delve into it, I will find
that all thoughts come from the one great mind.

But this one great mind is split in two,
and only the thoughts from Spirit are true.

The rest are based in fear and are untrue.
It is only from the ego that they spew.

The ego's thoughts are of sin and separation,
whereas Spirit's thoughts are of love and inspiration.

I must choose which of these to focus on,
for they will create the world that I gaze upon.

I'm Still at Home

I'm not at home in this world I see.
I'm not imprisoned here; I am free.

For as my mind is healed,
much more will be revealed.

I will experience great relief
as my mind is healed of false belief.

A psychic change is all that's needed
to be certain that love's sacred call is heeded.

So, of one thing I can be sure:
I'm still at home with God, innocent and pure.

The Oldest Trick in the Book

The oldest trick in the book
was when the ego bade us to look.

And what we saw, we thought was true.
It's what the ego hoped we'd do.

Thus, was our perception born
on that dark and fateful morn.

Our perception then formed our belief,
and from this first error we've had no relief.

But the darkness leaves when we turn on the light.
The ego resists this with all of its might.

"Choose again," says the Holy Spirit.
But we must be silent if we are to hear it.

It's with His eyes that we must look
if we wish to avoid the oldest trick in the book.

It Isn't Even Real

Spirit speaks to us, "It's your belief you must repeal,
for this world is all illusion. It isn't even real."

Be you no longer a victim of delusion.
Put to an end the ego's world of confusion.

For this you must learn if you are to heal.
It's all an illusion. It isn't real.

So there really can be no big deal
if it's all an illusion and it isn't real.

The truth of all Creation by the ego's world concealed.
The love of the Father for His Son shall be revealed.

Separation Is Not Real

If the seeming separation is not real,
and if it's this that the ego must conceal,

then these bodies are not real,
in spite of how they might feel.

And if these bodies are not real,
then let the bells begin to peal.

Let them ring out the message far across the land
It's the power of the mind to choose that we must
understand.

And if we have chosen sickness, then
Spirit asks us, "Will you not now choose again?"

Let us choose now to be one with God and His Creation,
for the power of our mind to choose is His new revelation.

The Road to Nowhere

How difficult is the journey to "out there,"
on the long, twisting road to nowhere?

The real journey is to look within
and find the belief in separation and sin.

To find and release it is what we must do
to let go of the false and accept what is true.

To believe in the dream of the many is not real.
To accept and believe that we are one is to heal.

Gratitude

Dear friends, please allow me the latitude
to express once more my deep sense of gratitude.

My former life was by no means a bad one,
but it seems as though I never had one.

Pain and loneliness did depart
as I lived with an open, full, and thankful heart.

And as I formed this new attitude,
I began to *feel* that deep sense of gratitude.

This may sound like just one more platitude,
but I am now filled with that deep sense of gratitude.

And I have chosen now to join the ranks
of those who live a life full of thanks.

I now count myself among the grateful,
no longer filled with thoughts that are hateful.

And I no longer despise myself,
for I've put those ideas back on the shelf.

I can take them down again if so I choose,

but I have nothing to gain and everything to lose.
So now I say to those who helped me,
"Many, many thanks, for I have eyes that now see.

And I have decided to cease my looking
and just to be grateful to know what's cooking."

Be Your Own Guru

(Read to the tune of "I'm My Own Grandpa")

Be your own guru.
Be your own guru.

It may sound silly to you,
but it's a thing you can do.
You can be your own guru.

Be your own guru.
Be your own guru.

You may not have a clue,
but if only you knew.
You can be your own guru.

Be your own guru.
Be your own guru.

It may be too much to chew,
but it's a goal to pursue.
You can be your own guru.

Be your own guru.
Be your own guru.

Don't get all in a stew.
Get a new point of view.
You can be your own guru.

Be your own guru.
Be your own guru.

You may think that you're through,
but there's much more to do.
You can be your own guru.

Meditation Writing III

I ask, "J, what would You say to me today?" His reply is as follows:

Greetings, My brother. This, the day that you have made, have fun and rejoice in it. While you are here in the dream, gather what enjoyment you can. Make love—that is, send love to all. Give all people their freedom. How else can you expect to have your own? Remember that whatever you give is what you receive. It is the great law of oneness! How can any part of the one not receive what is given? Allow what is to be! Give acceptance to all! And you will gain freedom! That is all.

Love,

J

Meditation Writing IV

I ask, "J, what would You say to me today?" His reply is as follows:

Greetings. Come, my brother, and join Me on the high road to heaven. Forgive *all* your brothers and sisters and their doings. This is the road home. How long do you wish to stay in this strange world, a world of constant domination over and condemnation of each other, a world of make-believe where everyone tries to exert control over others? How could anyone really have control over anyone else when there is only One? This world is a fantasyland where nothing is as it seems. Only love is real! Remember this always! That is all.

Love,

J

Be Happy

I'm happy or I'm thinking.
I'm happy or I'm right.

I'm happy or I'm sinking
into an endless night.

I've learned that it's a decision
to put an end to this division.

For if I put my trust in me, I'll be anxious, and I'll be
fearful.
If I put my trust in me, I'll be lonely, and I'll be tearful.

But the choice to be happy and let all judgment go
is to put my trust in Him and end the need to know.

The Monster in My Closet

While guilt and fear around me swirled,
I came to understand this is a nightmare world.

While I engaged in anger, judgment, and gossip,
I came to understand there is a monster in my closet.

This monster calls me by my name
as it fills me with regret, guilt, and shame.

But why not open up my heart, open up my eyes?
Why not let the love that lives within me rise?

Why not take on the Holy Spirit as my sponsor?
And why not at long last evict the egotistic monster?

Here Come the Judge!

Here come the judge! Here come the judge!
From his position he will not budge.

"Defend! Defend!" he roars, and he bellows
as he cries out against all of his fellows.

Filled with arrogance and righteous bluster,
with all the rage that he can muster,

he says, "Defendant, give me your plea,
for I am busy, can't you see?"

"Guilty," says he, as he bangs down his hammer.
"You are hereby sentenced to life in the slammer."

"For justice must be done
if I am to have any more fun."

But *my* safety lies in being defenseless,
in spite of the judge's harsh intenseness.

The judge is the ego, and he never lets up.
Criticism and blame are what fills his cup.

He can only be ousted from his position
by bringing forgiveness to its fruition.

Case Dismissed!

When by guilt we feel defeated
and from this life we have retreated,

the One who knows the truth steps in
and vehemently denies our belief in sin.

The guilt you have suffered is not for real.
There is no truth in it no matter *what* you feel.

For if you are brought before the higher court,
and if witnesses by the hundreds the charges support,

His Honor the Holy Spirit will insist,
the jury must acquit. Case dismissed!

Beware the Temptation

Beware the temptation to see yourself unfairly treated,
even if you feel betrayed, let down, and defeated.

Do not say to anything, "This should not be,"
and know that the body's eyes do not correctly see.

For what if all events were gently planned by one who's
on a higher level of being?
What if all events were gently planned by one who's on a
higher level of seeing?

What could you not accept if you only knew,
that all of this was being planned by one who knows
what's true?

Meditation Writing V

I ask, "J, what would You say to me today?" His reply is as follows:

Greetings, My brother. There is but one! This one is all that is. Everything is spiritual in its *true nature*. The world of the physical is the world of form. Spirit is formless. It is true, though, that spirit can be made to fit into any form. Then it *appears* that the form is real. Without spirit there can be no life in anything! Spirit is what gives life to any form. Spirit is at play in this physical world. And when the game is over, it returns to its home, just as a child returns home at the end of his playtime. That is all.

Love,

J

Meditation Writing VI

I ask, "J, what would You say to me today?" His reply is as follows:

Greetings, My brother. You are the lost one, trying to remember your way back home. And I am trying to help you to remember the way. It is in your mind, but you have forgotten who you are and how you got lost. It is all buried deep in your memory bank. You uncover it by refusing to take part in the dream of separation, by refusing to believe that a make-believe world is real, by refusing to follow the dictates of the ego. When the ego at last releases its grip on you, you *do* remember. This happened for Me, and so it will happen for you. I make you this promise! That is all.

Love,

J

Let Go!

Once we ask to be directed,
we learn much more than we ever suspected.

But to learn is not our only chore.
We're here to find much, much more.

Though we live our lives from May through December,
our *real* task here is simply to remember.

To remember who we really are
means to let go of what has brought us this far.

Only love is real, and the rest is naught.
Remember who we are. Remember whom we forgot.

Let go of blame and condemnation,
and find release from despair and frustration.

Let go of others and their wrongs,
and write *new* poems, sing *new* songs.

Let go of the future, let go of the past.
Live in the now; its dimensions are vast.

Let go of the ego's false belief,
and experience peace, joy, and relief.

Let go of the guilt, let go of the fear.
It's driving the dream; it's keeping us here.

Let It All Just Be

What I think upon does expand in my existence.
So why spend so much time in worry and resistance?

Why spend so much time in anger and in fret?
Why spend so much time in judgment and under threat?

Why does being right demand so much insistence?
Why not choose to be happy and do it with persistence?

Why not give up my rights and expectations?
Why not let go of blame and accusations?

Why not make the choice to be happy and be free?
And live a life of peace, merely letting it all just be.

Give Up Control

To connect with who I truly am, the soul,
I must be willing to give up all control.

For it's the ego that must be in control.
It wants nothing to do with the soul.

It wishes to be in charge of us all, you see.
My ego wants to have everyone love and admire me.

But the soul's agenda is to have me remember we're one,
to remember that I am not separate from anyone,

to remember that we are indeed whole,
and to give up all attempts at control.

It wants me to remember that our oneness is our one and
only goal.
It wants me to let go of the ego and follow the purpose
of the soul.

Meditation Writing VII

I ask, "J, what would You say to me today?" His reply is as follows:

Greetings, My brother. You need to take life in its present state one day, one moment, at a time. And you need to accept yourself, your surroundings, and your circumstances just as they are! To struggle with what is, is futile! You are not in control, and neither is anyone else. You are all at the mercy of the director of the great illusion. What is, is! And what will be, will be! This cannot be changed by you!

How will you deal with it? This is the great question. Will you choose love (acceptance), or will you choose judgment, anger, resentment, and fear? What you choose will determine what your next challenge will be! Love is the correct answer in all ways, in all things, and at all times. That is all.

Love,

J

Meditation Writing VIII

I ask, "J, what would You say to me today?" His reply is as follows:

Greetings, My brother. What you ask for is not to be given today. That is, what is wanted cannot be given. This is because you think you need something, anything, to make you happy. Realize that the only thing that can make you truly happy is to know that you need nothing to do that. You already have it! It is the power to choose. Choose to be happy! Choose to be loving! And ask My help. It is already in you. It only needs to manifest itself in your life. Wake up and know that the love and happiness you seek is who you truly are. Choose to be it *now*! I will help you if you ask Me.

That is all.

Love,

J

The Holy Spirit

What is the Holy Spirit?
If you listen for the answer, you will hear it.

"I am your friend. I am your guide.
I lead you back to God, from whom you hide.

I help you scale the highest peak.
I help you find the love you seek.

I lead you gently through the highest pass.
I am your teacher in the highest class.

I am the bridge between your dream and your true home.
I am your shepherd, from whom you need not roam.

Yes, I am deep within you, of that you can be sure.
And you remain as God created you—innocent and pure."

Spirit's Call

I am not a body. I am free.
For I am as God created me.

One self, united with Him.
Love overflowing, pouring over the brim.

I must see myself as He sees me,
an expression of love who is totally free,

free of all fear and free of all guilt,
free of the false world the ego has built,

answering Spirit's salvation call
by accepting and being forgiving of all.

Spirit's Class

In my later years in Spirit's class,
I had to learn this if I wished to pass.

The ego has been teaching me for years
to focus my mind on resentment, anger, and fears.

To change my mind is now required,
and by the Spirit I must be inspired.

Forgiveness is the holy preparation
for ending the ego's domination.

I must drop from my mind all thoughts of blame
if I wish to break free of guilt and shame.

And when I put forgiveness to the test,
anger and frustration are laid to rest.

To remember that we are whole,
I must set forgiveness as my goal.

Spirit, Let Me Be Your Light

Spirit, let me be Your light today.
Let me show my brothers the way,

the way to release the ego and its fear,
the way to find love in everyone here.

Spirit, let me be Your light today.
Let me find You in everyone along the way.

Spirit, darkness has held its sway
for far too long up until today.

So, Spirit, let me be Your light today,
and let Your light shine through me, I pray.

Meditation Writing IX

I ask, "J, what would You say to me today?" His reply is as follows:

Greetings, My brother. You have called upon Me to be your guide and your help. I will answer you by promising that I am always with you. You need merely ask My help in any situation, no matter how small and insignificant it may seem. There is no order of difficulty in miracles, and there is no order of difficulty in problems. Love (acceptance) is the answer to every so-called "problem." Accept what is. Accept all involved. Accept yourself and your present situation. This brings about the peace of God. And the peace of God is the way home to where I am. That is all.

Love,

J

Meditation Writing X

I ask, "J, what would You say to me today?" His reply is as follows:

Greetings, My brother. What is happiness? It is the lack of anything to worry or fret about. It is not money, financial success, fame, or power. It is not even having plenty to eat. It is being comfortable and free of judgment whenever, wherever, and however you are at the moment. This means not getting caught up in problems, whether they seem to be yours, others', or the worlds. Accept all! And be comfortable in spite of what is going on within you or without you. It is all of no consequence! Only love is real! Feel it and let it pass through you to others. It is the natural birthright of all! That is all.

Love,

J

God Is

They say that death is going through God's other door.
But we keep living on when the body is no more.

We say God is, and then we cease our speaking,
for we have found God's presence, and we can stop our
seeking.

And if everything that's real is very truly Him,
then the light of this false reality is very truly dim.

We say God is, and then we speak no more,
for this is the true reality at its core.

Nothing real can be threatened, and nothing unreal exists.
It's this great truth that the ego's world resists.

Herein lies the peace of God that we've been seeking.
Again, we say God is, and then we cease our speaking.

How Holy You Must Be

Think but how holy you must be,
from whom the voice for God calls lovingly

unto your brother that you may wake in him
the voiceless voice that speaks to him within

to finally free your brother from the ego's special reign,
to free you both at last from its weak and rusty chain.

For its hold on you both is only tenuous.
To break free from it really isn't strenuous.

A little willingness is all you really need
from its imprisonment to finally be freed,

willingness to see that you have been so wrong
and to follow Spirit back home where you belong.

Oh, how holy you must be
to finally set your brother free.

Thanks from God

Don't worry or fret. Be happy.
You have no reason to feel crappy.

Be grateful, be filled with joy.
Feel it bubble up; don't play coy.

Now's the time to open your heart and feel His great love inside.
Accept your thanks from God. You have never had to hide.

Presence

I am Divine Presence.
This is my true essence.

I must let go of the body's false identity.
I must accept that I am a spiritual entity.

I must let go of the belief that I am form.
I must let go of the belief that I must weather the storm.

I must let go of the belief that I am the mind.
I must leave all of these false beliefs behind.

Then what remains is only the observer.
And he is not the ego's life preserver.

He surely is God's pure essence.
He surely is love's pure presence.

In the Golden
Light of God

In the golden light of God,
in the golden light of God.

Peace and joy are in the air.
Love is flowing everywhere.

In the golden light of God,
in the golden light of God.

In love's pure golden light,
there is no place for guilt and fright.

In the golden light of God,
in the golden light of God.

And if I look at it, I'll find
That everyone is kind.

In the golden light of God,
in the golden light of God.

In God's pure golden light,
we erase the darkness of the night.

In the golden light of God,
in the golden light of God.

And when we all return as one,
the Holy Spirit's job is done.

In the golden light of God,
in the golden light of God.

Meditation Writing XI

I ask, "J, would You tell me how to rid this body of asthma?" His reply is as follows:

Greetings, My brother. Asthma is being short of breath. It comes from holding back your love. Love is the ongoing breath of life. Do not hold it back from anyone or anything! It is true that attacks are often brought on by allergies. Allergies are caused by resistance. Resist nothing! Go with the flow, even if it seems to be taking you somewhere you do not wish to go.

Just *know* that you are being led by Someone who cares for you! That is all.

Love,

J

Meditation Writing XII

I ask, "J, what would You say to me today?" His reply is as follows:

Greetings, My brother. This is a transfigured world when we approach it with love. Since all is created by thought, all we need to do is change our thinking. Simple? Yes. Simple but difficult in that the idea that it is our thoughts that create is so foreign to people. They think that their thoughts and the thoughts of others are privately held. And if they are creative, then why is the world in such a mess? They refuse to believe that their thoughts are so negative as to create this hell. It is all judgment (condemnation) of others, my brother, that is creating all of this. Try going without any judgment for any period of time, and you will see how difficult it is to change your habits of thought. But the good news is that it can be done.
The bad news is that it is your task to do it! Ask My help! That is all.

Love,

J

One with God

I know who we are, even if you do not.
We are one with God, even if you forgot.

To be one with God is to express His love and peace.
All our judgment we must now release.

For criticism and blame
only increase our guilt and shame.

And when we increase our guilt and shame,
we only prolong the ego's insane game.

God's Son Is One

The Son of God is my identity.
This body is, in truth, a nonentity.

God is but love, and therefore so am I.
And love is eternal; it cannot die.

The Son of God is only one.
His oneness cannot be undone.

As I forgive myself, I forgive my brother.
It must be so, for there is no other.

And love and acceptance, they are the same.
There is no one to glorify and no one to blame.

I look on myself and my brother as God's one Son.
And in my doing so, my journey back home is begun.

God's One Creation

If we give out love in each relation,
it's love we receive as God's one creation.

What I give to my brother is my gift to me.
For there's only one of us, you see.

It's essential that I give if I wish to receive,
for there's only one of us, I believe.

God's creation is only one.
We're each a part of His only son.

We truly are God's one creation,
not the ego's theme of separation.

God Is Within

God is not "out there" to be looked upon in wonder,
a voice to be heard within a roar of thunder.

God is to be looked upon and recognized within.
This is where our awakening must begin.

For if God is in you and God is in me,
there can be only one of us, you see.

And if we see only one,
our awakening has indeed begun.

Let us agree to see the face of Christ in each other
so that at long last His love we may discover.

Old Ideas

Old ideas will keep me stuck,
striving and straining and mired in muck.

These old beliefs never brought peace
but only suffering and guilt that never would cease.

I had to step out, get out of my box,
break open the lid, break open the locks,

try a *new* path, find a *new* way to think,
open my mind, forge a *new* link.

With the universe before me and horizons afar,
I must let go of the old and seek a *new* star.

For am I not one with all of the rest,
the poor and the rich, the worst and the best?

The power within me softly speaks,
"It's Me within all. The Romans *and* Greeks,

the Natives, the atheists, the large and the small,
they're all My creation, and I love them all.

And you My dear son, are one with the rest,
no better, no worse; you're *all* in My nest!"

Wholeness

His name denotes the nature of His being.
And *hallowed* means whole, a status that is freeing.

So, "hallowed be Thy name" tells us that He is whole,
not broken into pieces, each one bent on control.

And "whenever two or more are gathered in My name"
means that when the nature of love in each is the same,

then His wholeness has been acknowledged
and the mistaken belief in separation abolished.

And *holy* means whole as well,
a belief that will at last free us from hell.

The Witness

I am not a body; I am free.
For I am as God created me.

I am pure and innocent; I can do nothing wrong.
Total guiltlessness is my siren song.

I am not my thoughts, my feelings, my emotions.
I am not this body going through its motions.

I am not a part of illusions or of error.
I am not a part of nightmarish dreams of terror.

I am the silent witness, observing all around,
feeling all the feelings, hearing all the sound.

I sit behind the feelings, thoughts, and forms,
observing all the struggles, the violence, and the storms.

I am the audience of one, looking upon the scenes,
knowing there is nothing that any of it means.

Let Me Be Your Light Today

Lord, let me be Your light today.
Let the darkness of this world fade away.

Let Your light shine so others can see
that it is Your light that lives within me.

I know it will shine if only I ask it,
if I no longer hide it under a bushel basket.

If it lives within me, it lives within all others,
for am I not one with all my brothers?

Problems Are Us

The idea of a separate personhood
will always end up in no good.

It's the cause of all the fear and all the fuss,
because all of our problems are indeed us.

But when we experience our lives as one
is when we will have all the fun.

When we let go of the personhood
is when our lives are filled with His good.

We will live in love and peace,
and all of our problems will cease.

Gone will be our tears and our sorrow,
for our problems will all be gone by tomorrow.

God's Declaration

It is God's declaration
that there be no separation,

that in you lies His perfection,
that in Him lies no rejection.

It is the ego's insane plan
to do whatever it is it can

to increase our guilt and shame
and make us forget why it was we came.

So hourly remember why it is we came:
to bring the love of God into this children's game.

Meditation Writing XIII

I ask, "J, what would You say to me today?" His reply is as follows:

Greetings, My brother. All you experience in this life adds to who you are as you advance toward home. Make sure that love is the foremost quality you take with you in your bag of assets. Think love! Feel love! Express love! It is who *you truly are.* That is all.

Love,

J

Meditation Writing XIV

I ask, "J, what would You say to me today?" His reply is as follows:

Greetings, My brother. It is not for Me to take you home again. I cannot do that. It is for Me to show you the way home. You must make the final decision. But first we must clear away all the debris from the path. I can help you see it, and I can help you remove it. Call upon Me. I am here to help you with anything and everything. Open to love. Let go of the past and its many hurts. Hold nothing against anyone or anything. It never really happened anyway!

Pay no attention to what is going on out there. Pay attention to what is going on in here, that is, within your heart. Let go of the so-called "need" for anything outside yourself. It is your need to acknowledge the love within that is of paramount importance. Let go! Let go! Let go! That is all.

Love,

J

Stop Running

To rid myself of ego and merge me with You,
surrender is all that I really need to do.

For when this world of form I no longer see,
at long last I can be free.

From You I have been running away.
With Your love I now wish to stay.

My deepest desire is for all this running to stop.
I must let identification with this body drop.

Be You in Charge

This holy instant would I give to You.
Be You in charge and tell me what to do.

Tell me what to say and tell me what to think.
Lead me home to peace. Bring me back from the brink,

from the brink of disaster by following the ego mind.
Show me how to love, to be tolerant and kind.

Show me how to see Your presence in every being,
how to see this world as false through Your way of seeing.

I choose now to surrender; I step back at Your behest.
And I ask that You be in charge. It's my sincere request.

Meditation Writing XV

I ask, "J, what would You say to me today?" His reply is as follows:

Greetings, My brother. Your attention to detail is not needed to live and to grow. What is needed is discipline and perseverance. The first of these is lacking in you, but the second is strong and has served you well. Keep on keeping on with your studies and your involvement with recovery. Love is practiced well in AA. And your participation in *A Course in Miracles* is finally paying off for you. The love you learn is to be practiced in *all* situations and with *all* people. That is all.

Love,

J

Meditation Writing XVI

I ask, "J, what would You say to me today?" His reply is as follows:

Greetings, My brother. Your perseverance, as I said yesterday, is admirable. Make sure you use it in the service of God. Teach only love, for that is what you are. But teach it over and over until you become sick of doing it. Then do it some more. For *you* are in need of hearing it, and someone else may even hear it along the way. Love equals acceptance! This is what your world must learn. Accept *all* people, *all* situations, and *all* things! Do not resist anything! You will find that the quality of your experiences here will change as you practice this. That is all.

Love,

J

Don't Drop the Baby

To find peace is to fulfill Spirit's intent,
for if I find it, I can at last be content.

But then I must hold on as if it were a baby.
I cannot drop it no matter what the situation may be.

If I should loosen my grip on my peace,
I will cause this false world of form to increase.

And if it should then become my perception,
I will again be involved in the great deception.

For perception will surely become my belief.
And from this mistake there is no relief.

I shall once again believe that I'm special.
With this belief I must once again wrestle.

So, I must hold on to my peace no matter what may be.
Don't ever let it go. And don't ever drop the baby!

Finding the Peace of God

Now I seek, and I shall find,
God's eternal peace of mind.

To judge my brother for what he did not do
is to lose God's peace that is my due.

I must remember, in spite of what I feel,
that this world is illusion. It isn't even real.

God's eternal peace was given me at creation.
To find it through forgiveness is my true salvation.

To find the peace of God is now my urgent goal.
I know that all my brothers merely play a role.

Peace Is the Way

It's said that I should follow my bliss,
that I could have peace instead of this.

But how am I to ever find peace?
It's my old ideas that I must release.

My old beliefs that say we're not one
are keeping me here, ever on the run.

But if we are one, then who can I blame?
My condemnation of you brings *me* the feeling of shame.

Done again and again, it brought a deep sense of guilt.
A life full of anger and depression I'd built.

Now each new day, the skids I must grease
by vowing to do nothing that will not bring peace.

For peace is indeed the one true way
to change how I think, to change what I say.

And to change how I think alters my perception.
To see things differently puts an end to deception.

So, I am determined to see things differently today.
My priority is peace, for peace *is* the way.

Peace

I could have peace instead of this.
I could have love, and I could have bliss.

I could have peace in every situation
if I only I would give up my belief in separation.

If I give up ideas of guilt and blame,
if I give up ideas of pride and shame,

if, and when, I give up the fight
to always win, to always be right,

and if I give up all expectations
and all attempts at incriminations,

then fear and stress I will not miss.
And I could have peace instead of this.

Victim of Delusion

I have been the victim of delusion,
thinking that I could find happiness in illusion,

that I could find peace and love in hell
if only I could manage well.

This idea has once again brought me to my knees
with an intense feeling of unease.

I turn to the Holy Spirit now
and ask Him to release me from my secret vow,

to lead me into His world of peace
where I can at last find my true release,

release from the belief in separation,
and in this release find my certain liberation.

Journey to the Yucatán

As you set out for some time in the sun,
I hope you have a lot of fun.

As you journey through the Yucatán,
remember, *you* can do what the Buddha can.

Remember who you *really* are,
the child of God, His shining star.

And as you explore the Maya ruins,
hearing of their evil doin's,

their sacrificial rites so gory,
remember, it's all an endless story,

a story of sin and separation,
a story of quiet desperation,

a story of seeming individuality,
a false perception of our reality.

But think how holy you must be
to hear God's voice call lovingly,

"Psst, Kat, you must awaken.
It's all a dream; you've been mistaken."

God is incomplete without you.
He eagerly awaits your rendezvous.

Forgiveness is your ticket home.
It stirs your love so it may be known.

For love is what you *really* are.
Your belief in bodies is quite bizarre.

Please reveal your love today.
Are You Listening, Katherine Bray?

You can make a different choice.
You can follow Spirit's voice.

You can let go of the ego's hands
as you travel through these Mexican lands.

For you are the world's illuminating light,
shining away all the shadows of the night.

Please remember now why it is you came:
to bring the peace of God into this children's game.

You can remember your holiness
and let go of beliefs erroneous.

For when you remember we are one,
your work in this illusion can be done.

To all those who are reachable,
all those who are then teachable,

you can carry Spirit's word
that belief in separation is quite absurd.

So, until your return to our weekly meetings,
I send to you my loving greetings.

Until you once again return,
my love for you will ever burn.

Hourly Remember

The world goes with us whenever we take rest.
And all the sons of God are very truly blessed.

For when a tired mind is suddenly made glad,
a very weary soul in happiness is clad.

A bird with broken wings again begins to sing
and joyfully cavorts as if it were spring.

A stream long dry again begins to flow.
A world long dark again begins to glow.

So hourly remember the reason why we came:
to bring the peace of God into this children's game.

Meditation Writing XVII

I ask, "J, what would You say to me today?" His reply is as follows:

Greetings, My brother. You and I are on the same path with all others. We are on our way back home to our Creator. We all have the same goal, but we have chosen different roads to take us there. We will all arrive safely at the same place eventually. Following my path of nonresistance, forgiveness, and love will get you there more quickly. Try it! Practice it! And take note of the conditions of your life as you do so. You have already experienced the feeling of love on the increase within you. It will only come more often and in greater strength as you practice more. That is all.

Love,

J

Meditation Writing XVIII

I ask, "J, what would You say to me today?" His reply is as follows:

Greetings, My brother. All your struggles are for naught. Relax! Take it easy. I will see to it that you are taken care of. Place your faith and your trust in My love! It is what you are here to do. To express your love is to express God. Do not worry about *anything*! That is all.

Love,

J

Wake Up!

Life here on earth, they say it's illusion.
This sure leads to a lot of confusion.

Let go of the future, let go of the past.
Time is not real; nothing will last.

No future, no past? It's all a delusion?
This sure leads to a lot of confusion.

The world's a stage; it's all a great play.
We all play our roles; we all have our say.

Positive, negative, let it all go.
Float in the stream and go with the flow.

Resist nothing and no one, for it is said
that what you resist will find you instead.

"But what about guilt, anger, and fear?
Can't I keep them?" I said with a tear.

Why would you keep that which you dread?
Let go of it all! It's nothing, it's said.

For all that you see is not what it seems.
Wake up! Wake up! It's all in your dreams.

The Disguise

When once we made the choice to roam
and leave the safety of our Father's home,

we stepped into this insane dream
where nothing is as it may seem.

We invented this fantastic game
where we seem not to be the same.

But let us now make the choice to return
and experience the love for which we yearn.

And let us see the joy in our Father's eyes
when we drop this ridiculous disguise.

Dream Characters

Why give substance to a dream illusion?
Why give reality to a collective delusion?

Why believe in a dream that we have built?
Why take on a dream character's guilt?

The actions of a character in a dream
are not as drastic as they may seem.

For what is there in a dream that's real?
And what is there in a dream to heal?

Why not now choose to extend forgiveness to the One?
Why not accept atonement for myself and know my job
is done?

The Dreamer Is Me

I am not a victim of the world I see.
It's all a dream, and the dreamer is me.

I am love, spirit, and mind with freedom to be and do
whatever it is that I choose to.

The decision maker lies within me.
And my world is formed by what I choose to see.

If I choose to play the part of a separate being,
I'm free to do so by my way of seeing.

For my beliefs are formed by what I choose to see,
and according to my beliefs, so shall it be done unto me.

Is it not now the instant to choose to see anew
and create a different world by seeing what is true?

I am not a victim of the world I see.
For I create the dream, and the dreamer is me.

It's Only a Game

With all the spiritual teachings collected,
we'll find that it's true: we're all connected.

Where once we thought, *To each his own,*
we now learn that we're not alone.

After all the battles are over and done,
it's then we find that we're all one.

Who were we fighting on land, in the air, and at sea?
After years of seeking, I've learned there's just me.

For we are all actors believing our roles,
digging ourselves deeper and deeper in holes.

Filled with despair, frustration, and doubt,
we cry out in pain, "Please help us get out!"

And why has God not intervened?
Because, as He softly whispers, "It's not what it seemed."

Though we may whimper, laugh, sob, or scream,
He softly whispers, "Be still, My child. It's only a dream."

I search and I search for who is to blame,
while He softly whispers, "Be still, My child, it's only a
game."

Looking Inward

I look outside myself and see
a world that isn't so,

a world that has no guarantee,
a world I only think I know,

a world that shows me only duality,
a world of nightmares, a world of brutality.

But if I would only look inward, I would see
a world of love where I am free,

a world that's filled with happy dreams,
a world that's free of egoistic schemes.

So, I choose to look inward now,
and I hereby renege upon my secret vow.

Looking Within

Let me now live a day of peace, a day of joy,
a day that no annoyance can destroy,

a day in which I place all my investments
into a life that's filled with peace and acceptance.

For a life of peace and love can only begin
when I am at last willing to look within.

So, I will not fear to look within today.
In fearlessness and love is where I wish to stay.

This Children's Game

I am the Son of God, I am the Holy One,
acting out this play until my roles are done.

But I am not the roles I play;
I do not believe the words I say.

There must be another script;
there must be a better way.

For it is my desire to return from whence I came.
It is my deepest wish to bring an end to this children's
game.

A Flicker in Eternity

Life is but a flicker in eternity,
a short burst of flame, an uncertainty

in the world of the Spirit,
where we wish not to dwell, for we fear it.

Our true home is not in the world of form
where we are incessantly urged to conform.

These bodies are but a symptom of our belief in separation.
They hold us here because of our deep fascination

with the idea that they are real,
an idea that to us has great appeal.

But what if we were to let go of the idea that we are apart
and hold each other dear within our hearts?

Then love could make its long-delayed appearance,
and the ego could finally cease its interference.

Simply Ignore It

What do I do with this world of dreams,
one in which nothing is as it seems?

Spirit replies, "Just let it be.
For the real world is not the one you see.

The world you see is just a game.
To believe in its reality would be insane."

So, this world of dreams, do I then deplore it?
Again, He speaks: "Not at all. You simply ignore it."

Roller-Coaster Ride

We created this earthly amusement park,
having forgotten who we are.

We wanted to create a place away from God to run and
hide,
but we found ourselves on a fearsome roller-coaster ride.

First, we slowly crawl up to the mountain's crest.
Then rapidly we descend to the lower depths.

We then stretch and strain as we travel round the bend,
only to repeat the previous scary trend.

We loudly holler, and then we scream.
If only we'd remember that this is all a dream.

If only from this dream, we could be awaking
and put a stop to our fear and our endless shaking.

We Are Whole

The seeming separation never occurred.
To believe that it has is quite absurd.

To think that the whole has broken into pieces
is to place reality on what is facetious.

For it is quite comical, you know,
to believe to be real that which is show.

We are not these bodies we think to be real.
The belief that we are puts us through this ordeal.

To remember we are one is to awaken
and leave this world that we have mistaken.

So, let us repeal our once secret promise
and leave this world and all its dramas.

Sleepwalkers

We are all sleepwalkers, all of us blind,
in this vast game that we all designed.

What does it matter what we think, or say,
if we are all characters in our own play?

What does it matter if we laugh or scream
if we are all characters in our own dream?

And if this world is our dream of hell,
what does it matter if we fail or excel?

We are all beings of light, each one a great ray.
We are not the characters in these roles that we play!

The World of Illusion

All was well within the garden
until false beliefs began to harden.

For Adam and Eve ate the fruit of the tree
of the knowledge of good and evil, you see.

Prior to that, there was only One.
Now the world of illusion had begun.

And the concept of a you and a me
denied the real world of spirit and unity.

And once we perceived it to be,
we came to believe in its reality.

What the mind believes to be so
causes the false world of form to grow.

They feed on each other, form and belief.
From this first error, we get no relief.

But if all is one, there can be no reality
to the illusory world of form and duality.

Bless Them, Change Myself

By blessing them, I bless the world
and the flag of freedom is unfurled.

By blessing them, it will indeed change me,
for the real world is not the one I see.

The world of form is but illusion,
and I have been the victim of delusion,

that I could find happiness in this world of hell,
if only I could manage well.

But I am not the body that you see.
I am as God created me. I am free.

And those who seem to bring me pain
are not residents of this mad domain.

By blessing them, it is I who is changed.
And this world of the ego will be rearranged.

Can the Perceiver Be Perceived?

Can I go beyond what I've believed?
Can the perceiver also be perceived?

How deep must I go into this investigation?
What is the point at which I reach my destination?

When will I awaken from this illusion?
When will there be an end to this confusion?

When I move beyond the world of form's frontier
is when all these questions will disappear.

Disappearance of This World

There is one thing of which we can be sure:
for this sick world of the ego, there is no cure.

There are no ifs, ands, or buts:
this world of the ego is absolutely nuts.

And it's all our false beliefs that must be forsaken
if from this insane world of dreams, we are to awaken.

For when from our illusions we do at last wake up,
all we think we know will go through a shake-up,

and this false world will disappear from our sight.
We will finally return to our true home in the light.

Hallucination

Those who live in a world that is not there
often require psychiatric care.

And those who believe in hallucination
often require hospitalization.

Yet we who believe in this world as it seems
are unaware that it's all a product of our dreams.

We need only learn that we have been mistaken.
And all we really need to do is awaken

and remember what we already know.
We're asleep and dreaming of a world that is not so.

How Long?

How long, oh God? How long must it be
before we can see the way You see?

How long, my Father, how long must we strive and strain?
How long must we endure the suffering and the pain?

How long, my Creator, how long until we awake?
How long must we live out this mistake?

How long, oh God, until this game is done?
How long until we go back home as one?

It Just Doesn't Matter

Music by David Harrison and Brian Jones; lyrics by Brian Jones

It's all a big dream. It's all an illusion.
It's all a big dream, a gigantic delusion.

It's all a big dream.
It just doesn't matter at all.

It's not what it seems, for we will awaken.
It's all in our dreams; we've not been forsaken.

It's all a big dream.
It just doesn't matter at all.

Spirit tells us what we already knew.
The love of our Father is all that is true.

The rest doesn't matter, doesn't matter at all.
It's all a big dream that leads to confusion.
It's all a big dream without a conclusion.

It just doesn't matter.
It just doesn't matter at all.

I've Been Mistaken

I am not this body. I am free.
For I remain as God created me.

I am not this body. I am not this mind.
And if I look within, I'll surely find

that I am the witness to all these dreams.
I am the observer of all that seems

to be so true, that seems so real,
all that seems to be such an ordeal.

But why do I react to events in illusion?
Why do I persist in hanging on to delusion?

Why not let go of this false world and its charm?
Why not choose now to set the alarm?

For about this dreamworld I've been mistaken.
And from this dreamworld I will awaken.

Nothing Real Can Be Threatened

We have been fooled by the physical, it's said.
By its seeming reality we have been misled.

But nothing misleads us more than illusion.
We have been the victims of our own delusion.

For what we project, we then perceive.
And what we see is what we believe.

And what we believe then becomes real
in this false world with its insane appeal.

On and on we go, project and then perceive.
We observe, and then we believe.

We believe and then we project.
It's all a false concept.

And the appeal of this false world persists.
But nothing real can be threatened, and nothing unreal
exists.

Herein lies God's eternal peace,
where we can at last obtain our release.

The Other Road

As my previous take on life has unraveled,
I find that I've embarked upon the road less traveled,

the one that so many pass right by
as they proceed along on their way to die.

But this road leads to eternal life,
free at last from this world of strife.

This road leads to God's love and peace,
to a place where His wonders never, ever cease.

Why did it take me so long this road to discover?
Why did it take me so long the truth about myself to
uncover?

It is because I have been fooled by the physical.
It is because I have so long denied the mystical.

I've believed that everything must be scientifically proven,
and I've been the unwitting character in a gigantic
delusion.

But this, the other road, leads me back to where I really dwell
and out of this self-made prison, this vast dream of hell.

Our Soul's Purpose

Our soul's purpose is to finally wake up,
to put our dreamworld through its final shake-up.

But our sole purpose, our one and only aim,
is to finally concede that this world is just a game.

So, our soul's purpose is to remember who we are in truth.
Our soul's purpose is to have faith, not irrefutable proof.

Psycho Planet

If ever by chance
we should find ourselves in France,

then we'll know the dream of self has dared us
to set foot in the city of Paris,

to avoid this wonderful City of Lights
and keep us living in panic and fright.

What is our choice now to be?
To continue our belief in what we see,

or awaken from this state of delusion
and no longer give credence to this illusion?

For this psycho planet, the ego's nightmare dream of terror
has been brought about by our choice to believe in error.

This Darkened Land

Spirit, I ask you now to take me by the hand
and lead me out of this darkened land.

Release me from this dream of fright
and lead me now to Your world of light.

Relieve me from the need to be special.
Release me from this world so stressful.

I would trade this world of guilt and fear
for the world You hold to be so dear.

Please walk me out of this endless night
and show me now Your world of light.

The Tiny Mad Idea

Into the mind of the Son of God crept the tiny mad idea:
I think I'll dream up my own world, a veritable panacea.

Oh, this will be such delicious fun.
I'm going to separate from the One.

Laying all the truth of who He is aside,
He thought, *I'll have a place to run and hide,*

a place where I'll escape God's wrath.
And thus, the Son of God remembered not to laugh.

That dreamworld had such appeal,
He came to believe that it was real.

But now He's come to say, "Oh, for Christ's sake!
I'm asleep, dreaming that I am awake."

So maybe the time has come to let go of this mad scheme.
Maybe the time has come to finally awaken from this
dream.

Gnucci

Whatever happened to Gnucci, my old friend?
Was he merely a result of my efforts to pretend?

Or was he really there, my companion at play,
who watched me grow older and then went away?

He lived behind the fridge, you know.
But my parents treated him as though

he wasn't real, and they thought I would one day find
that he was only a character in my mind.

But now I have finally come to understand
that we're *all* characters in this game we've planned.

Must we all continue playing until we win?
Or can we remember that there is no guilt or sin

and thereby from this dream awaken,
finding that we are not forsaken?

Thanks to you, Gnucci, my childhood friend,
for showing me this whole world is just pretend.

Meditation Writing XIX

I ask, "J, what would You say to me today?" His reply is as follows:

Greetings, My brother. Your tendency to look, look, always look for the answers is taking you to where you need to go. Always look with an open mind. The answers will come. Do not be closed to anything! If what you find is not true, then you will be led to what is true. Keep looking. It has brought you this far, and it will take you even farther, to where I am. I await your return and that of your brothers and sisters. That is all. I love you all.

J

Meditation Writing XX

I ask, "J, what would You say to me today?" His reply is as follows:

Greetings, My brother. Your time spent in meditation is that of a serious seeker. Keep looking. Keep asking, and it all will be shown to you. Ask for love. Ask for peace. Ask for understanding. Ask for patience. I am here to be of help to all of you. But you must ask. That is all.

Love,

J

The Choice

We actors have chosen to go our own way.
"To hell with direction" is what we all say.

"Each one of us knows what's best for me."
Beyond our own nose, we're unable to see.

But the Author has written the plot and its bends,
and we actors don't know how it all ends.

The day will come when we end our roles
and return to our Maker as one, as whole.

For us the play will end, and we'll all walk away,
while our brothers audition for new parts in this play.

On and on the script extends.
On our beliefs it all depends.

But the final curtain *will* be drawn
when *we* no longer choose to go on.

The Game

Labeling, judging. When will it stop?
Top to bottom, and bottom to top.

Good or evil, clean or unclean,
better or worse; what does it mean?

The script has been written. The game has begun.
Forget who we are. Forget we're all one.

But even though dark clouds block it from view,
the sun is still there; we know this is true.

Have we forgotten that we are all one?
Have we forgotten the clouds hide the sun?

Part two of this game is to bring back to mind,
investigate everything, see who you find.

We need to remember that this is our goal,
to recall we're not separate, to recall that we're whole.

And when we remember, the clouds fade away.
The sun is then seen; the sky is not gray.

There's no longer a need to judge and to label.
For everything's open and out on the table.

There's no longer a call for blame and exclusion.
Acceptance of *all* brings the end to illusion.

Part three of this game is to live this belief
and in this find our joy, our peace, our relief.

The Watcher

You are but the watcher of this movie being shown,
so do not claim this character as your own.

Do not try to change events upon the screen,
for its but an epic movie that is being seen.

Do not say to anything, "This should not be."
For the body's eyes do not correctly see.

You are the presence in the theater, the audience of one,
the watcher of this movie ever since it has begun.

But understand that the watcher can leave at any time.
He does not have to sit and wait until the very last line.

So, make the choice now to step out into the light,
and let the watcher bring an end to this world of fright.

The Cowboy

I went to a cowboy movie the other day.
Everything the cowboy said, I heard myself say.

I saw everything the cowboy sees,
and I felt the same ache he felt in his knees.

I felt his emotions, his ups and his downs,
his anger and frustration, his smiles and his frowns.

I smelled all the smells that came from the herd.
And *I* felt a slight movement whenever *his* horse stirred.

I thought all the same things that the cowboy thought.
And I wore the same boots that the cowboy had bought.

I tasted his coffee, so hot and so black.
And I felt his warm sweat as it ran down his back.

I soon asked myself, "How can this be?"
Could I be the cowboy that I went to see?

Or am I a witness who merely took note
of all of the scenes that the screenwriter wrote?

I'm not too sure; it all seems so hazy.
If I think I'm the cowboy, then I must be crazy.

But wait a minute. I'm still wearing a ten-gallon hat.
God, please help me to understand that.

Cowboys and Indians

Cowboys and Indians, good guys and bad.
It seems that this is the only life I've had.

Cowboys and Indians; in which group do you belong?
My constant condemnation was my only song.

I saw everything in terms of right and wrong.
My constant condemnation was my only song.

Cowboys and Indians, a life filled with resentment.
Good guys and bad; I had no contentment.

After years of seeking, I've found there's but One.
I now say goodbye to cowboys and Indians, for a new life
I've begun.

God's Movie

This is God's movie, and He alone is real.
How does this sit with you? How does it make you feel

to know that you are but a part of some vast cosmic game
where nothing is for real and no one is to blame,

to know that in the wheel of life, you are but a spoke,
to know that you forgot to laugh at this cinematic joke?

It matters not at all what you think you've seen.
All events take place upon some movie screen.

To remember this is but a movie and that God's the only
thing that's real,
is to finally wake up and put an end to this ordeal.

At the Movies

We each appear in the Projectionist's light
on this vast movie screen each day and each night.

Why worry and fret about problems we see?
We're all in this movie about you and me.

When we leave the movie, do we hate the villain
for all the bad things and all of the killin'?

The actor is not as bad and as mean
as the character he plays upon the screen.

And the actress is not really the great queen
that she portrays in each royal scene.

We know it's not true and that none of it occurred.
We knew that when our roles we procured.

It only seems to be true
from our distorted point of view.

So, like in the movies, we only *play* our roles.
It's not who we are. We're one; we're whole.

So, let's make one thing perfectly clear:
there's really nothing in the movie to fear.

Charade

Spirit, please induce my mind to heal,
and let me get off this ever-revolving wheel,

this wheel that returns me here life after life after life
to the ego's world of worry, suffering, pain, and strife,

the ego's world that is so skilled at concealing
that it's my mind, not my body, that needs a healing.

So please put a stop to this never-ending parade.
Awaken me to your world and bring an end to this
charade.

The World's a Stage

Shakespeare said this world's a stage.
It's filled with scenes of laughter, tears, and rage.

We are the actors in this play.
We don't really mean the lines that we say.

And we have forgotten who we are.
From our true home we have wandered far.

We have believed ourselves to be filled with guilt
because of the scenes in this play that we've built.

But hear this now, a word to the wise:
there is only the actor, no good or bad guys.

And we must forgive ourselves for what we did not do.
For plays are not real, and scripts are not true.

What Dreams We Do Dream

Proudly proclaimed on our magnificent marquee,
put up in lights for everyone to see:

Now playing on the stage in this theater,
starring all of us, the sons and daughters of our
Creator:

What Dreams We Do Dream:
Life as It May Seem.

We cast the actors in the roles that are assigned.
We dress them in the costumes that we alone designed.

We write the script, and we cue the lines.
It's we who determine who it is that shines.

And it's we who will decide to draw the final curtain
when we choose to follow Spirit. Of this we are certain.

The Driver

Those who wish to recall may need our assistance
to remember who they are, to seek with persistence.

But for those who won't seek, our assistance won't work.
They'll just believe we're some new kind of jerk.

But by observing the changes He's made in us,
they may want to know who's driving the bus.

To know it's not me who's driving this bus
brings a new freedom, eliminates fuss.

Stop telling the driver which turns to take,
when to speed up, and how often to brake.

For it is He who steers my course today.
It is He who writes the lines in this play.

It is He who directs the acts and the scenes.
It is He who provides the ways and the means.

To invite this gentleman in is what's needed.
But without sincerity, my request is not heeded.

And once He comes in, He will not stay
without a new invitation on every new day.

I ask Him to direct my thoughts every day.
And I observe the new scenes that appear in this play.

I react with wonder as I live each new page
and see the new actors who emerge on this stage.

But all is decided by the Driver, of course.
It avails me nothing to try to use force.

It's Just a Play

I know it doesn't seem that way,
but this whole world is just a play,

a world in which I forgot
my lines, the scenes, the entire plot.

To me it seems like such a shame
that this whole world is just a game.

But it's all a grand delusion,
and this whole world is just illusion.

In spite of how it all may seem,
this whole world is just a dream.

It's a world of false duality,
a far cry from God's reality.

For God created only one,
and then His work was done.

But this *one* had a tiny mad idea:
"I'll create a universal panacea,

a world where I can run and hide,
a world of pain, and guilt, and pride,

a world in which I live and die,
a world in which I justify

everything I do and say.
For I've forgotten it's just a play."

Characters in the Play

Our sinlessness protects us from all harm.
There's no need to view this false world with alarm.

We're not these bodies. We're not the characters in a play.
We are as God created us, whole, pure, and innocent in every way.

We never did the things they did. *We* never said the things they said.
We're merely the actors playing out our roles instead.

And so, it is too, that we are free of guilt and shame.
For the actions of the characters, the actors are not to blame.

So, let us remember now who it is we really are.
To believe we are the characters is really quite bizarre.

It seems we've left our home in heaven, but it's only in our dreams.
We're still at home with God, where His love forever beams.

The Cast Party

When the curtain has rung down and there's an end to
this vast play,
the actors and the audience will all cry, "Hooray."

The tyrannical king will remove his crown,
and the scheming queen will take off her royal gown.

And all of us will hurry, so as not to be tardy,
because we all wish to attend our cast party.

For, you see, we are not the characters that we portray.
This whole world is merely a Shakespearean type of play.

And we actors are not sent to a heaven or a hell
just because we all played our parts so well.

So, let us all be grateful; let us not be sorry.
Let us all rejoice and take part in our cast party.

Let's Not Pretend

Is it really true that we intend,
to live a life we only pretend?

To play with toys that we misconstrue,
to make them say and do what we want them to?

To get caught up in this silly game
where we are filled with guilt and shame?

Is it not now the time to awaken
from this dream that we have mistaken

to be real and true,
where we are victims of what others do?

Let us choose now to put away our toys
and stop this game that only destroys.

And let us now cease to play in a world so fractional
and return to our home, where our unity is actual.

Life of Brian

Once upon a time, I lived the life of Brian,
or as it seemed to me. I am not lyin.'

But this person Brian is but a character in a dream.
And the entire story is but the ego's scheme.

It is a story of separation, a story of personhood,
a story of blame and guilt that does no one any good.

I now let go of every story, every false belief,
in order to obtain Spirit's everlasting relief.

Journey without Distance

We've been on this journey without distance
through the ego's world of resistance,

resistance to characters in a dream.
How insane it all does seem.

Please help us turn loose of this mad role.
Wake us up and make us whole.

Our Big Mistake

The character in the play urges the actor to awaken.
"Wake up, wake up, for you have been mistaken.

This character is not who you really, really are.
You're much more than this, much more by far.

To remember who it is that's really, really you,
a little willingness is all you need. There's little else to do.

For you are the one formed by the Creator,
not the many characters portrayed in this theater.

So, wake up, wake up, for pity's sake,
and come to realize you've made a big mistake."

Tell a Different Story

Don't be cruel. Don't be unkind.
Open your heart and change your mind.

Tell a different story; just begin.
Tell a different story than the one you're in.

Let go of your tale of sadness and dejection.
Let go of your tale of pain and rejection.

Make it a story of light and love.
Make it a story of being above

this battleground of hate and sin.
Tell a different story than the one you're in.

To Shirley

Here's to the woman I loved so many years ago,
the one who chose to let our marriage go.

Here's to the woman I loved to touch,
the one who put me through so much.

She's the one who pushed me to the brink.
I knew no other way; I had to turn to drink.

She acted out her role so very, very well.
I sunk down into my own private hell.

Here's to the woman who brought on all the pain
without which I would have made no gain.

For I had to find a different way to live.
And I had to learn a different way to give.

I had to let go of anger and resentment
to find a life of peace and contentment.

I had to forge a relationship with God
and give the spiritual way of life a nod.

So, here's to Shirley as she goes through her transition.
She played a huge role to assist me on my mission.

Meditation Writing XXI

I ask, "J, what would You say to me today?" His reply is as follows:

Greetings, My brother. Take My word. You are love, free from all guilt, anger, and fear. You *are* free of all negative influence so long as you practice love, forgiveness, and nonresistance. You were not created to live in fear and guilt, and neither was anyone else. There is no one else. You and I and all that is are truly one in spirit and in consciousness. Oneness is our very essence. And that One is truly free, pure, and innocent because love is its very nature. That is all.

Love,

J

Meditation Writing XXII

I ask, "J, what would You say to me today?" His reply is as follows:

Greetings, My brother. It is for you to make the choice to return home now. It is for Me to show you the way, to hold your hand, and to accompany you along the path. Turn to the Father in *all* things. He will provide so long as you remember Him as your Source. The path is one of love, not judgment.

Remember this! Practice it! And it will naturally become your way of life. Is it possible that it could be better than what you now have? That is all.

Love,

J

Actions of the Insane

This world is small, ridiculous, and absurd.
It's the craziest thing of which I've ever heard.

Brilliant actors playing roles that are inane
throughout this epic play entitled *Actions of the Insane*.

We enter on the stage and assume our new parts
with the goal of always coming from our hearts.

But as we play out our mad game, we may come to find
that all our decisions have been coming from our mind.

We continue our crazy roles on stage until our parts are ending.
Then we make our exits with doom and gloom impending.

But our entire future is nothing but a return to the past.
For this play will run again, but with another cast.

A World That Is Insane

Stop trying to make sense of something so inane.
Do not try to attach reasonableness to a world that is
insane.

Stop trying to link effects to their cause.
Quit delving into this world that never was.

Be content with this world and its way.
Why be concerned with events in a play?

Acceptance is the answer to all your problems today.
All that occurs are but scenes within this play.

There is no guilt, no punishment, no shame
attached to any moves you may have made within this
game.

Insanity

It's clear that all of humanity
is caught up in this world of insanity.

In this world of dreams where nothing matters,
all of us are mad as hatters.

And we're all late, we're late,
for a very, very important date,

a date when we'll awaken from the deep
state of slumber that we call sleep.

At last to awaken and no longer fear it.
Our return to our true life as spirit.

Grievances

Grievances hide the light of the world in me.
I must let it shine if we are to be free.

I must see no fault, no guilt, in my brother.
I must recognize that there really is no other.

For after this game is over and done,
I know I'll find that there is only one.

And this world of form cannot be all that it seems
if the entire thing is a product of my dreams.

Holding a grievance is to react to dreams of fantasy,
and reacting to dreams is a form of insanity.

I'll end up believing that it's true
if this dreamworld I misconstrue.

And if I believe that it's all fact,
then what really is true I have attacked.

I need to respond with acceptance and peace
if from this dream we would gain our release.

I Need Help

Be in my mind, Spirit, throughout this very day.
I welcome Your direction as to what to think and say.

For, have I not been a victim of the delusion,
that I could manage well my life in this illusion?

I urgently ask Your direction as I wander through this valley
where the shadow of death *seems* to be the grand finale.

But death itself is a part of this insane illusion.
Please bring me home. Bring this mad dream to its conclusion.

Meditation Writing XXIII

I ask, "J, what would You say to me today?" His reply is as follows:

Greetings, My brother. You are to be commended for passing My message of love and acceptance to others. Now it is time to pass it on to your own inner self. Tell him it is now time to love and accept himself. It is now time to end all resistance.

It is now time to recognize yourself as one with God and with all others. This is the key, the answer to *all* problems, the way out. You are worthy of it, and so are your brothers and sisters. That is all.

Love,

J

Meditation Writing XXIV

I ask, "J, what would You say to me today?" His reply is as follows:

Greetings, My brother. Judgment can bring no good to anyone in any situation. For all judgment is an attempt to make someone "special." Either you condemn them for not being as good as you think you are, or you admire them for being better than you think you are. *No one is special!* How could anyone be "special" if there is only the one? And be assured that there is only one of us! We are all a part of the whole, just as all fingers are part of the hand and no one finger is any more "special" than any of the others. They each have their function as a part of the hand. How can one wave in the ocean be any more "special" than any other? You get my point? *Do not judge!* It is the chief block to the awareness of love's presence. That is all.

Love,

J

Forget the Past

Let me forget my brother's past today,
and let me set him free to find his way

back home, from where he never drifted
through the happy dream from which he can be lifted,

raised up to oneness with a higher power
where love and peace and joy still flower.

The Past Is Over

The past is over. It can touch me not.
But the belief in the past is fraught

with feelings of fear and guilt and sin
when I take for real this world I seem to be in.

For the ego would keep me delving into the mystery
of what never really happened in our history.

So, let me forgive all those events that did not really occur,
and let me forgive all those persons who never really
were.

Let me now turn loose of my belief in the past
and set us all free of fear, guilt, and sin at last.

Time Is Nothing

The past is nothing; it is no more,
like the vague outline of a distant shore.

The past is nothing, and it never was.
Time is nothing, and this is because

it's something we made a useful tool.
It's something we made in order to fool

ourselves into believing that this world is real.
It helps to give this false world its appeal.

The future is nothing, and it never will be.
Time is nothing, and this is the key:

to release ourselves from guilt and fear
and thereby cause God's world of love to appear.

Our Treasured Wounds

Why hold on to these wounds that we so treasure
throughout time without measure?

Why do we insist that others listen
as we endlessly recount our rendition

of all the events that made us what we seem?
To put the blame on others is the ego's insane scheme.

But why not let go of our painful past
and find God's endless peace at last?

Why not put our painful past to rest
and by God's eternal love be blessed?

We Must Forget

We must forget the language of the ego,
the one that is with us wherever we go.

The language of damnation, criticism, and blame,
the language of disgrace and remorse, of guilt and shame.

We must forget if we are to call back to mind
the language of Spirit, with which we are aligned.

The language of love, the language of forgiveness,
the language of acceptance and nonresistance.

We must forget the language of separation
if we are to assist the Holy Spirit in His preparation

for our exit from the ego's world of extremes
and our entry into Spirit's world of happy dreams.

So, let us now forget the language of our past
in order to remember who we are at last.

Meditation Writing XXV

I ask, "J, what would You say to me today?" His reply is as follows:

Greetings, My brother. You are on the right track. Stay there. Investigate everything and accept what rings true to you. But don't resist anything else. This play, this game, this illusion, this dream, that you are taking part in is not being orchestrated by you. You cannot change anything except how you see it, that is, how much of your energy you give to what is not true. If you invest your energy in what is not true, it makes it seem as if it is true, and this perpetuates the whole mess. Withdraw from it. Be in the game, but don't be *of* it. That is all.

Love,

J

Meditation Writing XXVI

I ask, "J, what would You have me know today?" His reply is as follows:

Greetings, My brother. All is one. That is all anyone *ever* needs to know. Because all is one, nothing can be done to, for, or against anyone. Whatever befalls one person occurs to all people to one degree or another. Therefore, live in love, peace, and joy. Do it not just for yourself, but for all. There is no other way. That is all. I love all of you. How could it be any other way? If I love one of you, I am loving all of you because you are *not* separate.
Again, all is one.

J

Nothing Matters!

As I slept soundly, free from my mind's endless chatters, the voiceless voice spoke to me, "Nothing matters! Nothing matters!"

Only a murmur to begin,
it grew louder and louder, this voice within.

Finally, it left me with no doubt.
"Nothing matters! Nothing matters!" It increased to a shout.

At last I was woken
by these strange words the voice had spoken.

It made no sense to me.
Nothing matters? How could that be?

But what if this world is just a game?
Then nothing and no one is to blame.

And who is it that must be made to pay
if we are all actors and this world is just a play?

And who is it that garners all the glory
if this world and its events are merely a story?

Nothing matters! And *no one* is at fault!
And there are no hurdles that anyone must vault.

Innocence

What can be the effects of a dream,
no matter how realistic it may seem?

We are still the one that God created.
From Him we've not been separated.

Nor have we been made apart from our brothers.
For there is only the One; there are no others.

Loving spirit is who we really are.
We're not a part of the ego's insane repertoire.

This world and all its horrific incidents
cannot destroy us or our innocence.

So why not love the only one that exists?
For as long as we fight it, the ego's world persists.

I Must See Your Innocence

I must see your innocence, my brothers.
I must see the innocence in all others.

I must see your innocence, pray tell,
to realize that it is mine as well.

For what is in one must be in the lot.
And there is not one who is forgot.

So, innocence is what we all must be.
And guilt and shame I must not see.

The Truth

The guiltless mind suffers not
as we call to mind what it is that we forgot.

It's Him in whom we live and have our being,
in spite of the separation we think we're seeing.

The thought of anyone being guilty
is absolutely, very silly.

For verily and forsooth,
we are one. And that's the truth.

Meditation Writing XXVII

I ask, "J, what would You have me know today?" His reply is as follows:

Greetings, My brother. You are love—all of you. Know this! Think it! Say it! Build it into your deepest place. Quit looking for it. You *are* it!

This is the great dichotomy. You are looking everywhere outside yourself for what has always been inside you. When you really find it inside, it will also be everywhere you look outside. That is all. I love *all* of you.

J

Meditation
Writing XXVIII

I ask, "J, what would You say to me today?" His reply is as follows:

Greetings, My brother. It is time for you to join wholeheartedly in the effort to free all of you. Let go of all attempts to make this illusion real by letting go of the ego and its feeble attempts to create the impossible. Let go of all belief in guilt and separation. We all are one, pure and innocent. We are not guilty, we never have been guilty, and we never will be guilty. This dream you are engaged in is a dream of guilt and punishment. *No one* is ever to be punished, because *no one* is guilty of what never happened. Do you not see this? That is all. I love you all.

J

The Hush of Heaven

The hush of heaven holds my heart today.
The incessant blather of the ego no longer has its way.

The raucous clatter of the ego mind,
once love has been embraced, is left far behind.

And the ego's constant criticism,
which often hides behind witticism,

is silenced by God's eternal peace
as love for my fellows is on the increase.

It's then I can forgive them for what they did not do.
It's then I can finally let go of all that is not true.

It's All Untrue

My goal is to be all that I can be.
But I must let go if I am to be free.

Let go of the future, let go of the past.
Let go of the guilt that keeps me aghast.

Let go of demands on how it should go.
Let go of it all, all I think that I know.

Give up my insistence on life as it seems
with a new understanding: it's all in my dreams.

Forgive my brothers and sisters for what they did not do.
Forgive myself, for it's *all* untrue.

My Sinless Brother

My sinless brother is my guide to peace.
And from this false world I would gain my release.

I now choose to forgive my brother for what he did not do.
From this false world of pain, I would like to be through.

I now take my sinless brother by the hand
and let him lead me out of this godforsaken land,

lead us both back to where we started,
to our one true home from which we never departed.

On this journey without any distance
to a land of dreams, of nonexistence.

It seems we've left our home in heaven, but it's only a
painful dream.
We're still at home with God, where His love and peace
forever stream.

The Old Ball Game

Ever since the beginning,
you've awaited your big inning

when you would awake
and this false world forsake.

Take your place now as Spirit's pinch hitter,
and spoil the ego's no-hitter.

Take your turn now at the bat
and let go of all that

which you think you know.
For in truth it isn't really so.

Step up to the plate,
and let go of your hate.

Be willing no longer to defend.
Bring this extra inning game to its end.

Now go and hit your home run
by truly forgiving everyone.

True Forgiveness

To look on you, judging your misdeeds,
being gracious by overlooking them misleads.

For forgiveness is only true
when I forgive you for what you did not do.

In this awareness will I also see
that what I did not do will also set me free.

I then realize that in an illusion,
all our misdeeds are merely delusion.

It's then that I take you by the hand
and let you lead us both to the promised land,

to the land of the happy dream
where God's love will forever beam,

where He can lift us up and take us home
to His dwelling place, from which we need not roam.

Meditation
Writing XXIX

I ask, "J, what would You say to me today?" His reply is as follows:

Greetings, My brother. All you have learned and all you are learning is contributing greatly to your return home. Begin writing poetry again. I will help you if you ask for My help. Writing poetry is a lovely way to learn and to help others learn. Be true to yourself, to who you truly are: God's love in expression within the dream. When you finally awaken from the dream, that is what will remain: God's love in expression outside the dream. That is all. I love you all.

J

Meditation Writing XXX

I ask, "J, what would You say to me today?" His reply is as follows:

Greetings, My brother. It is paramount that you recognize and accept the holiness of your brothers and sisters—all your brothers and sisters. For it is their oneness with the Father that makes them so. When you pray, view them all as the recipients of your wishes and desires. And be grateful that this is so. Not one of you is better or worse, higher or lower, because you are all a part of the One, as am I. Whatever you wish for anyone is a wish for all. Therefore, keep your thoughts, your desires, your prayers, on the high level of spirituality. No one can be separated from the wholeness, that is, the holiness of all that is! This is the great fact. All is one! No matter how much anyone desires it to be different, it remains so. That is all. I love you all.

J

In the Deep

Wherever we are, wherever we go,
it's hard to be rid of persistent ego.

The ego cries out, "See me! See me!
I'm the smartest, prettiest wave in the sea."

But how can a wave be apart from the sea?
It fools itself, crying out, "Look at me! Look at me!"

Swirling and crashing, and roaring its might,
it proudly proclaims, "I'm right! I'm right!"

It's about separation, and this is its song:
"I'm right! I'm right! I'm right, and you're wrong!"

Rolling and breaking, all covered with foam,
unaware of the stillness beneath, unaware of its home.

But upon its demise, washing up on the shore,
the smartest, prettiest wave of them all cries out no more.

For the ego, the false one, has been put to sleep.
And the glorious soul joins itself in the deep.

The Ego's World

Into the ego's insane thoughts I have bought,
and this crazy world is what I've wrought,

the ego's world of seeming reality
and its endless story of false duality,

a story of suffering and pain,
a story filled with strife and strain.

It's a story filled with guilt and fear.
Why would anyone wish to stay here?

The Ego's Evil Brew

God's love, peace, and light are shining in me now
as I choose to renege upon my secret vow,

the vow to ever follow the ego's dark and dreary plan
and never see the light that dwells within the man.

Never to look upon the love and light within,
never to look beyond the ego's world of sin.

I now look upon the actor, not the characters in this play.
I know we can be free. Forgiveness is the way.

So, I forgive us all now for what we did not do.
And I drink from Spirit's cup, forsaking the ego's evil
brew.

Ego or Spirit?

The ego is about separation, you see.
It makes me believe there's a you *and* a me.

While Spirit teaches that we are all one.
When we remember this, His task is all done.

But the ego puts up a mighty fight.
It needs us to think that we're always right.

It brings us to conflict, worry, and anxiety.
And when I am anxious, I'm trusting in me.

Anxiety only increases all fear,
while reliance on God beckons Him near.

But the ego is a tenacious parasite,
feeding on its host all day and all night.

Not knowing its host, on leaving this sphere,
destroys its playground, leaving nothing for it here.

So, I must choose now which one to follow,
Spirit or ego—one solid, one hollow.

To follow the ego is surely insanity.
Its reasons for living are pride and vanity.

I now select Spirit—it's loving and kind—
and let go of the ego, chase it out of my mind.

What of the Ego?

What of the candle who thinks it is the sun
and never knows its light is from the One?

And what of the ripple upon the ocean's crest
that never knows it's one with all the rest?

And what of the snowflake that thinks it is the storm,
never knowing its demise will occur if it gets too warm?

And what of the cloud that thinks it is the sky,
never knowing it will fade if it ever goes too high?

And what of the ego who insists we are apart
and from our unity with love would have us depart?

And what of the love that seems to ebb and flow
while we grasp at hanging onto its soothing afterglow?

Above the Battleground

Oh, how I'd love to live above the battleground,
where peace, love, and unity abound.

High above the ego's world of struggle, fear, and strife
where I seem to be doomed to return, life after life.

Above the ego's world of guilt, remorse, and shame,
above its insane chase for superiority and fame.

Above its murder and abuse; all as the ego planned it.
How can we all remain upon this psycho planet?

Today I look upon its anger, rage, and war
and finally decide I'll return there no more.

Avatar

If I am judging, then I am in hell.
And I know this oh so very well.

When I judge you, it is me who suffers.
I must climb out from underneath the covers.

I must see you as the love you really are
and remember that each of us is an avatar,

A divine teacher representing Spirit within our dreams,
in order to wake us from the ego's insane schemes.

So, I choose to leave the darkness and to judge no more.
Today I choose to walk through heaven's bright door.

Deception

If I but look within, I may find
that there's only the one great mind.

And this mind into two parts is split.
And if I am honest, I must admit,

the one part is of the ego, and it is loud.
The other is of spirit and is endowed,

with love and acceptance, compassion and grace.
I must now choose which part to embrace.

For it constantly feeds me a thought,
that either brings me peace or makes me distraught.

I've accepted the ego's thoughts, and I've been deceived.
I am not the thinker of these thoughts as I've believed.

Hatred

The ego speaks: "I must have someone to hate, you see.
It keeps you from being all that you were meant to be.

Oh yes, my hatred is expressed through you,
unless you block it from coming through.

You are my pawn. I use you to keep you ignorant
of your oneness. You must think you're different.

I must keep you in the dark, completely unaware,
so that to your seeming separation you would swear.

And if in your separation you would falsely believe,
I can keep you blinded to the truth. I must deceive.

For if to your oneness you would awaken,
then I must disappear, completely forsaken.

So, please do not open heaven's loving gate.
Find someone to judge as different, someone to hate."

I Am Determined

I am determined to change the way I see things,
to experience what a focus on only love brings,

to let go of who I think I am, to let go of what I think I see,
to let go of the ego's insane scam, and to be all that Spirit
sees in me.

It's Up to Me

I am not a victim of the world I see,
for I choose what I perceive. It's up to me.

I am the dreamer of the dream,
the chooser of what I see,

the architect of my esteem.
It's up to me.

I can take part in the ego's plan of attack and defend,
or I can follow Spirit's plan. On Him I can depend.

I can be imprisoned by the ego, or I can be set free.
It's all in what I choose. It's up to me.

I can choose the ego's frightful world to see,
or I can choose the oneness of Creation. It's up to me.

This Dusty Road

I have grown so tired and weary
on this dusty road so dreary.

On a journey without distance,
I *need* your guidance and assistance.

For I'm feeling abandoned and alone,
left by those who have stayed at home.

I'm feeling sad and disconnected.
I'm feeling unloved and rejected.

While frustration and despair, like clouds around me spin,
the despotic ego looks on with his ghoulish grin.

Won't You please rescue me from this endless hell
and provide me with Your healing, make me well?

Won't You lead me now into Your happy dreams
and save me from the ego and its insane schemes?

You Have the Power

Judgment, guilt, and fear are etched in solid granite
as we play out our insane roles upon this morbid planet.

From the reigns of pharaohs, czars, and kings,
our painful song of torture rings.

From dungeons, prisons, and jails,
one can hear the mournful wails

of we, the incarcerated beings,
with our incessant pleadings.

"Please, let us out," we vainly implored.
Our unrelenting prayers seemed to be ignored.

But Spirit speaks with His voiceless voice,
"All you need do is to make a different choice.

You have the power to obtain your release.
There are no locks, and there is no need for keys.

Follow Me," the Holy Spirit asks,
"and leave behind the ego's world of tasks."

A Faulty Decision

This entire affair is merely a game
with ego and Spirit both staking their claim.

We made a faulty decision in the beginning,
believing that the ego's plan was the way of winning.

This desire then prompted the power of One
to provide the evidence, to show it as done.

Situations and people then appeared in our dreams
and led us to accept this world as it seems.

Our acceptance resulted in giving it credence.
This world of the ego exists only in pretense.

Our belief in this false world then causes the One
to bring us more evidence that we have indeed won.

This cycle remains in effect to this day.
To renounce our decision is to finish this play.

Is It Not Myself?

Who is it that heaps upon me their trash?
Who is it that could be so brash?

Why must I pay for their transgressions?
Why must I dispose of their possessions?

The ego shouts, "This isn't fair!"
It tells me to defend. I must prepare

for another's attack upon me.
Is there not another way to see?

Is it not myself who leads me through this prison?
Is it not myself who lives this life without Spirit's vision?

Is it not myself who has saddled me with affliction?
Is it not myself who drives the nails in my own crucifixion?

I must listen for His voice to say, "Wipe all the sweat from
your brow.
Love and accept yourself just as you are right now."

Goodbye

Let's now say goodbye to this world of guilt,
goodbye to this world the ego has built.

Goodbye to this world of criticism and blame,
goodbye to this world of depression and shame.

Goodbye to this world of fantasy, this world of delusion.
Goodbye to this silly game, this world of illusion.

Goodbye to this play and its insane themes,
goodbye to this world of nightmarish dreams.

Goodbye to a world of judgment and resentments,
and hello to a world of His love and acceptance.

The Ego's Defeat

Love and forgiveness are all that is needed
in order to see the ego defeated.

For the ego relies on our guilt and our fear
in order to keep us reappearing here.

To see ourselves as part of God's pure light,
Places the ego in a state of fright.

And for the ego, that is the ending.
No more attacking and no more defending.

No more loneliness, no pain of separation.
No more hopelessness, no more desperation.

No more judging and being apart from.
At last to unity and love will we come.

Meditation Writing XXXI

I ask, "J, what would You say to me today?" His reply is as follows:

It is written that we are one. This idea can be found in all the major spiritual teachings of this world. If it were not so written, there would be little hope of ever finding it out. It is the function of the Holy Spirit to place that teaching where it will most likely be found by the masses. Even then, many will not believe that is so and will resist it mightily. But resistance to the truth does not alter the truth. It merely prolongs the time it takes you to awaken to it. All that is required is a small amount of willingness to open the door for your return to Truth. See to it that you retain the willingness to see yourself awaken. Be vigilant for God and His forgiven world. That is all. I love you all.

J

Meditation Writing XXXII

I ask, "J, what would You say to me today?" His reply is as follows:

Greetings, My brother. Follow My lead. Let it take you where it will. I promise that it will not take you anywhere you do not wish to go. Deep within your soul is the remembrance of your home, a place of love and light. Your deepest desire is to reside there consciously, a true place of refuge from this world and its ongoing storms. You will find peace there. You will find love there. Make the choice to return and ask Me for My help. It is My job to show you the way. I will accompany you, and I will hold your hand as you ascend the very same ladder you once descended to come here. That is all.

I love you,

J

Who Do You Think You Are?

Who do you think you are?
To even ask the question seems bizarre.

Don't we think you know?
But what you think; it isn't so.

You were created in His image and likeness,
filled with His love and kindness.

You are not a separate being, not a body.
You are not a part of this false world so shoddy.

If you were created as one, as whole,
who is it that needs to be in control?

And if you were created a being of light,
who is it that insists on being right?

If you were created one with Him,
you are filled with love to the brim.

You are not a part of violence and war.
You are not a part of egos galore.

So, who do you think you are? If only you knew.
You're one holy being of light and love. And that is what
is true.

This Idiotic Tale

This entire world of form is an idiotic tale
told by an amnesiac in an imaginary jail.

It's filled with terror, guilt, and war.
Why do we keep coming back for more?

It has no meaning. It's taking us all nowhere.
It's filled with insanity and rage. Why do we go there?

It's because we've been mistaken. We've taken it for real.
And we pass it on to others with passion and with zeal.

Let us now teach only love, for that is our true being,
and silence this idiotic tale that keeps us from truly seeing.

The Prodigal Son

I found myself walking down a dark and dreary road,
overburdened with a huge and very heavy load,

a load of sin and guilt and fear and shame,
a load of resentment, of criticism, and of blame.

I went on and on this way until I hit my bottom,
filled with frustration and despair, totally downtrodden.

And although I had refused to believe in His existence,
I turned to a higher power and asked for His assistance.

He urged me to turn around and walk the other way,
where love, forgiveness, and compassion were at play.

He said He would throw a party upon my returning,
for His endless love for me had been forever burning.

And before I reached the halfway point,
He promised that He would not disappoint.

And then I knew I'd trodden this path of the prodigal son
into the regions of hell and now back home to the Holy One.

Acceptance

Acceptance is the answer to my problems today.
Love and acceptance are my *new* way.

For if I'm upset, my serenity has flown.
Resentment and anger are the seeds that I've sown.

And these seeds that I've planted will bloom and they'll grow.
So I must be vigilant and practice what I know.

When I accept you, it's *me* I set free.
In place of my judgment, I just let you be.

Acceptance and approval are not the same.
Acceptance just means I don't have to blame.

And a life without blame will bring *me* peace.
From resentment and anger, I'll get *my* release.

Acceptance of *all* is the new life He's built.
And a life of acceptance says goodbye to guilt.

Truth Comes from the Heart

All deception seems to come from within my head.
I need to listen for the truth within my heart instead.

For by the "knowledge" of others I seem to have been misled,
by all that they have written and all that they have said.

I know God has spoken by the love I feel inside.
I need to let my feelings be my one and only guide.

I need to turn away from all I think I know,
for if I feel no love, it's certain it's from the ego.

And it doesn't require some great sleuth
to know that my heart tells me only the Truth.

To Love or to Judge

To love or to judge, our choice is clear:
to return to our home or remain here.

Here in this world of pain, fear, and sorrow,
the pain of the past and the fear of tomorrow.

We could choose to go home to a world of peace
when our brothers we forgive and thereby gain our
release.

Let us hold our brothers sinless, and we are then healed.
For our unity and innocence is at last revealed.

It's God's Love

Love cannot be divided into parts.
It's the one love of God that we feel in our hearts.

It's God's love in all its beauty
that teaches us that acceptance is our duty.

And it's God's love that fills my being,
regardless of the insanity that I'm seeing.

It's God's love that fills me up.
And it's God's love that runneth over my cup.

And it's only God's love that I feel,
for it's only God's love that is real.

This Ancient Wanderer

I have been filled with resistance
on this journey without distance,

this journey back home to the place I never left,
on an endless, senseless journey totally bereft

of the knowledge of the love that I am.
Now, from a journey through a world of bedlam,

come I, this ancient wanderer of rhyme,
back home to know the love I am for the very first time.

There Is No World

There is no world, there are no bodies, no time, no space.
We're not at home in this world of form; we come from
another place.

It is a place of peace where we're calm and joyous,
a place of endless love with nothing to annoy us.

Let us choose now to leave this world of constant
condemnation
and return to the place from which we came, home to
love's emancipation.

River of Life

Dedicated to Joyce and Barry Vissell and their Shared Heart Foundation
This song came to me in a dream.

What is this river of life but flowing freedom?
What is this river of life but flowing love?

When emotions are blocked, your river is stopped.
If you want to be smart, just open your heart.

Flowing freedom,
flowing love.
If you want to be free,
let it flow to the sea.

If you want to feel free, you must open the gate.
If you want to feel love, let go of your hate.

Flowing freedom,
flowing love.
If you want to be free,
let it flow to the sea.

If you want to feel joy, you must feel your pain.
If you want to see the sun, take a look at the rain.

Flowing freedom,
flowing love.
If you want to be free,
let it flow to the sea.

If you want peace at last,
let go of your past.
If you want to start anew,
just begin by loving you.

Flowing freedom,
flowing love.
If you want to be free,
let it flow to the sea.

May You Be Blessed

May you be blessed, O morning star, in all your glory.
May you be blessed as you play your role in this story.

May you be blessed as you recall
the tiny mad idea of it all

when all the morning stars sang together
as we embarked upon this daft endeavor.

May you be blessed, O beautiful morning star.
May you be blessed by the love that you are.

Master or Slave

Master or slave: which shall it be?
This is the story of the last century.

Make them all bow down. Keep them in tow.
If I give them their freedom, who knows where they'll go?

Crack the whip. Make them obey.
If they step out of line, there'll be hell to pay.

Show them who's boss, not the one filled with fear.
If they know I'm afraid, they'll laugh and they'll jeer.

And I'll be exposed for the man I've become,
Cruel and unkind, self-centered and numb.

Then a *new* master will throw *me* a bone,
and I will be stranded, afraid, and alone.

I *must* give up all of this fear
'ere disaster comes perilously near.

For who appointed *me* to this throne?
I assumed this great power all on my own.

And that which I greatly fear will come upon me
as surely as great ships sail the vast sea.

There are only two questions, I need ever ask:
"What would love do now?" and "*Who is it* behind the
master's mask?"

The Guardian
at the Gate

Here I stand on duty, the guardian at the gate,
to turn away all thoughts of fear, guilt, and hate.

But once in a while, one of them creeps in
and urges my return to a belief in sin.

I check them all for the proper ID,
for they have the power to create the world I see.

But I welcome in all thoughts of love, forgiveness, and compassion,
for I know that they create the world that God would fashion.

So, I stand on duty around the clock, 24/7,
for my devotion to duty opens the gates of heaven.

The Dash

Between the dates of my birth and my demise
lies the dash, how I lived this life in my disguise.

How often did I live a life of love and kindness?
How much was I affected by the ego's blindness?

How well did I accept this play as it was plotted?
How much did I resist the love that was allotted?

How often was I gentle, compassionate, and forgiving?
How often was I aware of the life that I was living?

It's not too late to change the way I view others.
It's not too late to see them as my sisters and my brothers.

Blame or Heal

All situations serve only to awaken us
from the false sense that there is a break in us.

But we remain as fashioned by our Creator,
even while playing all the roles in this theater.

And these roles we play are not real.
We must become aware of this to heal.

We must refuse to heap on others all the blame.
We must not take on the character's guilt and shame.

For we can cast all the blame, or we can heal.
We can make love the only emotion that we feel.

Adventure in Loving

It's said that there is nothing
as rewarding as this adventure in loving.

And our reason for being here
is to extend His love so dear.

Our only purpose for living
is to simply be forgiving.

For this entire world of form is not true.
And we must forgive everyone for what they did not do.

No matter what it is that we may face,
our job is to spread God's love and accept His grace.

Your Presence

It is your presence that begins to warm my heart.
And then this bubbling up of love begins to start.

As I gaze into your deep, deep eyes of brown,
the love within me starts to pound.

And as my fingers touch your lovely hair of gray,
this voice within me pleads with me to stay,

to stay within reach of your presence so dear,
to stay within reach of your presence so near.

For by your presence I am smitten,
and by love's presence I've been bitten.

We Never Left

The seeming separation never really occurred.
From our at-one-ment we never really stirred.

No matter what we perceived to be so,
there is no other place to which we can go.

We've been on a journey without distance,
within a body that has no existence.

And regardless of the appearance that we did roam,
we remain at rest in His love, in our true home.

We Are Worthy

I am surrounded by the love of God.
There's no need to continue with this facade.

For this much I have learned:
the love of God cannot be earned.

The love of God is found within.
There is no separation; there is no sin.

Our value was established by God at our birth.
We need do nothing to prove our worth.

Warriors of Love

We have entered this world, and we have found
that we are the protectors of hallowed ground.

The longer we are here, the more we find
that this hallowed ground is the field of our mind.

This mental field has not been easily won.
There have been many obstacles to overcome.

So, we stand as guardians at the gate
to turn away thoughts of fear and hate.

For we are the warriors of love,
here to give the ego's thoughts a shove.

This Strange World

In this illusory world that seems so strange,
we must give up the need to change,

to find that change was not our need,
but to remember we are divine indeed.

This must be our one and only goal,
to remember we are one, we are whole,

not divided into seemingly separate parts.
We must awaken to the love within our hearts.

Our belief in this world of dreams merely prolongs our
ordeal,
for in this world of illusion, only love is real.

Staking Our Claim

Today we say goodbye to shame and guilt,
goodbye to this house of cards we've built.

For in the absence of guilt lies our innocence and purity.
And the memory of our unity with God is at last a surety.

In the absence of guilt and shame,
we can then stake our claim,

our claim to His love and peace,
our claim to our final release.

The Sentry

I am the sentry, ever on watch to seek and find
the one whose thoughts are trying to enter my mind.

Are they from the ego, the one who would deceive
by flooding my mind, controlling what I perceive?

Or do they come from the Holy Spirit?
The sentry must stay alert to hear it.

For it is what and how I perceive
that determines what it is I believe.

And it's my belief that governs the conditions of my life.
Is it filled with love or with sadness, tears, and strife?

I must allow only those thoughts to get through
that speak of love, for its only love that is true.

Seated in the Lap of Love

While seated in the lap of love, feeling we have been rejected,
we dream that we are not worthy, feeling sad and dejected.

But how can we awaken from this dream?
How do we let go of this unbecoming theme?

We gently awaken to our oneness with Creation
and let go absolutely of our belief in separation.

We turn away from blame and condemnation.
We let go of all attack and confrontation.

We loosen our grip on guilt and fear,
and we finally get that we're not even here.

Programming

Our operating system is nothing but love
preinstalled at our birth by the Great Spirit above.

It's been built like a cork that will float to the top
unless something else has forced it to stop.

What can it be that makes love so outmoded?
It's other programming that *we* have downloaded.

Judgment and fear, resentment and guilt:
they're all essential to the structures *we've* built.

They're heavy, and keep our corks suppressed,
only rarely allowing our love to be expressed.

Let us delete them all now, and let our corks float up,
allowing our love to flow and fill *everyone's* cup.

For this is our purpose, to let our love flow,
and *feel* it fill our hearts with its compassionate glow.

My Birthright

Today I know that I have a choice
if I listen to the still, small voice

that speaks of there being only the One
and tells me my return home has begun.

It speaks of only my innocence
and urges me to maintain my vigilance

and listen only to its voice so dear—
and make the choice to persevere.

So today I choose only love, light, and life,
instead of the ego's pain, suffering, and strife.

Today I gratefully accept the love, life, and light
that is already mine, my divine birthright.

My Precious Child

My precious child so dear,
let me make one thing perfectly clear.

I have always loved you, for how could I not,
even if for a period of time I had forgot

that I am divine, and so are you.
Of this I had not a clue,

I knew not that we are made in the image of Him,
especially when our light seemed to be so dim.

And the Divine is love; of that I am sure.
Both of us remain innocent and pure.

We need do nothing to prove our worth,
for it was established by Him at our birth.

Kindness

My mind is a receiver; my heart is a giver.
Its message of love is my job to deliver.

No matter what thoughts of fear may enter my mind,
I need to respond with love; I must be kind.

For kindness to my brother will transform this dream.
It will undo my connection to thoughts of the ego's regime.

Isle of You

When I was young, I set my sail and headed due west true.
'Ere long, I came upon the lovely, lovely Isle of You.

I fell in love with the lovely, lovely Isle of You,
lush and verdant, under beautiful skies of blue.

Deeper and deeper I fell for the lovely Isle of You,
covered in beautiful blossoms everywhere in view.

It matters not how you say it; its meaning still rings true.
The lovely, lovely Isle of You says that I love you.

I Am the Light within You

I am the light within you.
Our oneness is what is true.

I am not a separate being.
Oneness is Spirit's way of seeing.

You are the light within me.
I choose now through Spirit's eyes to see.

But the ego tells me I have personhood.
This false belief leads to nothing good.

It keeps me chained within this prison cell.
It keeps me reliving this experience of hell.

But I choose now to release myself from this dungeon.
And I choose now to give up all my ire and my dudgeon.

For I am the light within my brother.
And we are the light within each other.

And God is the Father of all this light.
It is His love that will end this world of fright.

I Am Not a Body

I am not a body; I am free.
For I am as God created me.

A being of light is who I am,
no longer taking part in the ego's insane sham.

I am spirit and oh so free,
no longer to play the role of who I thought was me.

I no longer choose to continue this mad portrayal
in the ego's insane world of death and of betrayal.

Yes, I am spirit, alive and oh so well,
no longer to exist in this ego-constructed hell.

I am spirit, and it's by love that I am healing.
At last the peace of God is what I'm feeling.

Yes, I am spirit, alive and on my way
back home to God. And that is where I'll stay.

Horse Behind the Cart

I have put the horse behind the cart.
For from this body I am quite apart.

I've seen this body as who I am.
But I am the witness; this body's just a sham.

It is my mind that needs to heal.
This body isn't even real.

I am love's presence in this false world of duality.
For love must be present even in a world that has no reality.

Love is present everywhere, even in a world of dreams.
And God is but love, regardless of how it seems.

For love is deep within me, within my very being,
covered by blocks to my awareness of its presence in my
seeing.

Who it is I thought was me,
was this body that cannot be.

So, I must not put the cart before the horse.
From this body I must get a divorce.

The Greatest Gift

The greatest gift I could ever give, you see,
is to simply let you in to love me.

Love is meant to blossom and to grow.
And love is meant to freely flow.

To shut out love is not my goal.
My purpose is to know love as whole.

For love is who I really am, who I really must be.
And it must be shared; it must flow free.

But if I continue to build this wall,
I will never feel our one heart's call.

And if look inside as I've dared,
I'll find that all our hearts are shared.

The Bubble

In the lake of life, I am but a bubble.
So, what's the problem? What's the trouble?

A bubble rises from its murky past
toward the surface of the lake so vast.

Then the bubble bursts and is no more,
merely to be replaced by another from the floor.

The bubble, upon bursting, leaves only the waters of the lake,
where there is no more fear of rejection, misery, or heartache.

The bubble rejoins all that ever was
where there is no more effect, no more cause.

Only peace and love exist within the deep,
where I can at last awaken from this sleep.

Ancient Wisdom

Let us hear again the ancient wisdom
that first we must seek God's kingdom.

For His kingdom is none but love,
and it is this that we must seek thereof.

And since we receive all that we give,
to spread His love is how we must live.

For our lives are about our relationships with others.
They're really about how we touch our brothers.

So, let us remember that no matter what the question,
to love our brothers now is God's suggestion.

And if God is all that is,
what could there be that is not His?

If with God's love we can now ourselves attune,
we'll find there's really no one else in the room.

Where Is the Love?

Where is the love that I've been looking for?
All the while it's been knocking at my door.

At last in me it did confide,
"I've been knocking from the inside.

"Let me out! Let me out," it cries.
"For I cannot go on living these lies.

I've been made to freely flow.
I've been made to go where I must go."

Love cannot be inert forever.
It must be included in every endeavor.

What Is Love?

Love is gracious, love is kind.
And if I seek it out, I'll find

that I am love and love is me,
regardless of what you think you see.

You are love and love is you,
no matter what you say or do.

We are love and love is us,
even if we drink and cuss.

Love is the nature of our being,
even if from it we seem to be fleeing.

Why not stop and welcome its gentle kiss?
Why would we run from love's eternal bliss?

Love is genuine. Love is real.
It fills my heart and changes how I feel.

Love is the true nature of our being.
It is the very soul that it is freeing.

We Are Love

Could this be the end of a long, long line
of lives that seemed to be yours and mine?

We are not in control of our lives, you see.
We only pretend that's how it should be.

We're all engaged in self-deception,
and it's been this way since our inception.

Our lives are *really* His to have and to hold,
through thick and thin, through hot and cold.

For He is the actor playing *all* the roles;
He is the director filling *all* the holes.

These lives of ours, they ebb and flow.
Like a soap opera, on and on they go.

They rise and they fall as they use up their power,
while we sob and we moan, and in fear we cower.

We see *everything* bloom, flower, and fade
while we live our lives lonely and afraid.

If only we knew we are *not* these roles.
We've forgotten we're one, forgotten we're whole.

Our egos refuse to look at this One.
They keep us here, searching for fun,

always reaching for just one more thing,
hoping in vain for the love it should bring.

But the love of the ages was not ours to lose.
If we look very closely, we'll find it wearing *our* shoes.

For love is not something we must get to live.
Love is the one thing we *really* must give.

He is but love, and therefore so are we.
And in our knowing of this, we are finally free.

True Love

Does true love live only in a song?
Does it only once in a lifetime come along?

Did I only read of it in a poem?
Or could it make *my* heart its home?

Did it just briefly come along my way,
to tinker with my heart, to take my breath away?

Did it capture my heart and make my head feel light,
only once or twice on a beautiful moonlit night?

Or could it now fill my eager heart with joy
and make me once again feel like a little boy?

Could it much more than a moment last?
Could it make me forget the future and the past?

Could this be lived throughout the eternal now?
If this could only be so, please show me how.

Oh, how I long to hold it in my arms,
to feel it fill my heart, to feel its many charms.

To run my fingers through its long, soft hair,
to feel its warm glow, and to know it's always there.

I now make this heartfelt plea to the one and only Poet:
please make this happen now so *I* may really know it.

Teach Only Love

Teach only love, for that is what you are.
This is the highest teaching there is by far.

Lay aside your robes
and rise from the judge's seat.

Refuse to judge today.
Accept everyone you meet.

Stop fighting everyone and everything.
See what the return to sanity will bring.

Love your God, your neighbor, and you.
This is all you really need to do.

The rest is mere commentary.
To live a life of love is what is necessary.

Only Love Exists

We're taught that only love exists,
although the dream of fear persists.

Fear is only false evidence appearing real.
It's not the warmth of love and its appeal.

We've forgotten everything's all right.
We've forgotten we're beings of love and light.

So, let's remember now who it is that we must be.
We're one with all that is, more than human eyes can see.

Only Love

We are not these bodies that we see.
For we are still what God created us to be.

Only love. It's innocent and pure.
Only love. It's the only thing that's sure.

In this phony, phony world of dreams,
where absolutely nothing is as it seems.

What we must remember if we are to heal,
is that love, and only love is real.

My Little Cup of Love

When I was a young boy, my little cup of love never got filled.
The field that love had planted in me never got tilled.

I reached my young manhood filled with resentment.
I knew nothing of peace and contentment.

After suffering years of loneliness and pain,
and constant fighting and going against the grain,

I got weary and sick of trying.
I was tired of living and scared of dying.

It was then that I cried out to the One I couldn't see:
"God, if You are there, won't You please help me?"

I received an answer so long, long ago,
but I didn't recognize it until the years began to flow.

New friends and acquaintances pointed me in the same direction.
I followed their advice and began to live a life of introspection.

I commenced to look within to find the reasons for my grief,
only to learn at last that it was brought on by my belief,

my belief that love was something that I had yet to earn,
that there was something out there that I had yet to learn.

And I did learn one fact that I have come to face:
it was in me all along, a lovely gift of God's grace.

Love

Love—it's a feeling for the ages,
for the composers, the poets, and the sages.

It's a feeling that warms the heart,
that inspires music, poetry, and art.

It's a feeling that brings us close to each other,
that brings us to see everyone as our brother.

It's a longing to feel others so close and so dear.
It's an inner aching to hold them so near.

For love speaks to us of our oneness.
It brings us out of our state of numbness.

It tells us to let everything else go,
everything we think we know,

and asks us to accept everyone and everything,
and behold all that sanity will bring.

It's a feeling found deep within,
a call for our awakening to begin.

Love Is

Love is mine, love is yours, love is ours together.
Love is mine, love is yours, love is ours forever.

Love is not doomed to wither and to die.
Love is planted in our hearts to blossom and to fly.

To kiss each and every being that it may light upon.
Love is not a dash or sprint; it is indeed a marathon.

Love is within us all; it's deep within our very being.
Love is our only chance to leave this illusion that we're
seeing.

Love Is All We Really Need

Love is all we really need,
for love is God's own sacred seed.

We must not take our love for granted.
We must make sure that it's been planted.

For love is what will bring us back
from this mad world of guilt and attack,

back home from this mad world of shame,
back home to the place from which we came.

For love is all we've really needed.
And we must be certain that it's seeded.

Love Is Kind

Love is joyful; love is grateful.
Love is not judging; love is not hateful.

Love is patient; love is kind.
Love pays no attention to the mind.

Love accepts and lets us be.
Love is gentle and sets us free.

It frees us from a world of resentment.
It brings us a world of contentment.

For love is compassionate, love is forgiving.
It's not just a word; it's a whole way of living.

Love Is My Goal

Love is my only goal.
It's only love that makes me whole.

While the world around me believes in magic,
I must understand that this belief is tragic.

It keeps me stuck within this game
of constant judgment, guilt, and shame.

It prevents me from awaking.
It keeps me at God's will forsaking.

But happiness is God's will for me.
When I accept that, happiness is what I'll see.

And happiness is what I'll feel
when I learn that only love is real.

So it is that love is my only goal.
For it's only love that feeds my soul.

Love Is the Glue

Love is the eternal glue that binds us all together.
Love is the holy clue that we all live forever.

Love is the great adventure that we must all go through.
For love is the one and only thing that is forever true.

For the love that is within us, the love that we allow,
let us all be ever grateful, be ever grateful now.

Love Is What We're Yearning For

Drop your guard. Make no defense.
Forgive yourself. Tear down your fence.

For love is what we're learning.
Love is what we're yearning for.

Change your thoughts and change your life.
Heal the world, and end all strife.

For love is what we're learning.
Love is what we're yearning for.

Feel the love, receive the love.
Give the love, be the love.

For love is what we're learning.
Love is what we're yearning for.

Let love flow; let freedom ring.
We're all one. As God we sing.

For love is what we're learning.
Love is what we're yearning for.

Love Is Who I Am

Love is who I am, the whole of me.
For I'm much more than anyone can see.

I am a divine part, a portion of the One
Before time and space had even begun.

And I am as grateful as ever I can be
that this love, this One, is also inside me.

For what God has created as the One
cannot be divided, cannot be undone.

Love or Fear

It is said that only love exists,
although the belief in fear persists.

Yet what is there to fear
when the love of God is near?

And of what is there to be afraid
if there are no dues that must be paid?

It is in the absence of fear
that love must certainly appear.

It is only fear that keeps love suppressed.
Once love is freed, it must be expressed.

Love Sees Only Innocence

Love sees only innocence.
In its world, guilt has no existence.

For guilt is not real, although it seems to be,
in this dramatic production that we all want to see.

But if the peace of God is what I want to *feel*,
I must let go of guilt and shame, because they are not real.

Only love is real. Everything else is not.
It's this I must remember, for it's this I have forgot.

And I feel the love of God moving within me now.
It's put me at ease; it's soothed my furrowed brow.

And I am ever grateful, as ever as I can be,
for this wonderful feeling that's now come over me.

Love What Is

To argue with life is really quite mad.
It makes me angry, and it makes me sad.

A life that's filled with expectation
results in years of agitation.

To think that I control this mad illusion
only perpetuates this dream of delusion.

So, let me now put an end to confrontation
and finally put an end to expectation.

To love what is, is what brings peace
and a life of serenity that will not cease.

You Are Tremendously Loved

You are tremendously loved. Can you accept this?
Can you let this love pull you up and out of the abyss?

Can you invite this love to fill your heart and soul?
Can you remember who you are, the one who is whole?

You are tremendously loved. You must open up and let it in.
Release yourself and your brother from all guilt and sin.

You are tremendously loved. Open up and let yourself feel.
You are tremendously loved. Open up and let yourself heal.

Caught in the Web

It's about time, this phony world of dreams.
It's about space, this phony world as it seems.

It's about judgment, criticism, and blame.
It's about our separation, our guilt, and our shame.

We seem caught in the web of our own making.
And we tremble, for in fear we are quaking.

The way to break free of this web is to see Christ in our
brother.
What we see in our brother, we see in ourselves, for there
is no other.

To remove the blocks to our awareness of love's presence,
this is our purpose—and this is our essence.

For we are beings of light, each one a great ray.
To see love and light in our brother, this is the way.

Heaven's Song

If it's in love that I would believe,
then it's love that I must receive.

And if love's my reason for living,
then it's love that I must be giving.

And I must let go of all I thought I knew
to see the love that lives in me and you.

It's then I will march to heaven's song,
and in this world, I will see no wrong.

The Master

If I followed all the rules that I'd been taught,
then love would be mine, is what I thought.

And when things didn't go the way I thought they should,
I believed that if I tried harder that they would.

But my teacher didn't know the path,
and I laid on those others all my wrath.

I need a new teacher, one who knows the highway,
so I can stop trying to do it all my way.

Could I then have peace instead of all this?
Could I then know love has not gone amiss?

I now let the Master take my hand
and gently guide me to the artist's stand.

I now ask Him to paint the next scene
upon the artist's canvas screen.

For it's He who knows where all this leads.
It's He who knows my deepest needs.

It's He who knows the river's twists and bends.
It's only He who knows how all this ends.

I now let Him guide me on my way.
What have I got to lose? That's what I say.

The ego has led me far away
from where I was meant to be on this day.

The ego has told me I must be the best,
that I must be better than all the rest.

It's only then that I would be loved and accepted.
And all those others would be excepted.

There are no others is what I've learned.
And God's great love, for which I've yearned,

never left me as I wandered astray.
It's been deep inside *me* all the way.

My Offering

Giving is the same as receiving. That's what they say.
So, I offer to you my acceptance on this day.

I offer you my peace as you go along your way.
I offer you my love upon this very day.

I offer to you my kindness, if I may.
I offer you my gentleness in the middle of the fray.

I offer you forgiveness for the role that you must play.
For I know the script sets forth the lines that you must say.

And it's the director's commands I know you must obey.
So, I offer understanding without any more delay.

Today Is the Day

Fear and guilt are the ego's tools.
And he would have us look like fools

if we would follow Spirit in search of our home,
on this psycho planet never more to roam.

But today is the day to let go of the ego's hand.
Today is the day for love to make a stand.

Today is a day of love. Let me extend your love so dear.
Today belongs to love. Let me no longer live in fear.

Today is the day to take my brother's hand
and through my forgiveness, let him lead me out of this
insane land.

'Tis the Season

'Tis the season to be jolly,
and I will if it kills me, by gosh, and by golly.

For this season is not about nursing a grudge.
Let's give all resentments a shove and a nudge.

Let's hear the piano and sing the old songs.
Let's truly forgive everyone's wrongs.

Let's recapture our old youthful scene
with lots of red ribbons and a tree of green.

Let's once again feel all the love
that lives in us, a gift from above.

Let's soak in again the old Christmas spirit.
Let's open up to feel, see, and hear it.

For it is not presents and wrappings that we seek
but a loving embrace and a kiss on the cheek.

We can't take with us the gifts we were given.
Our only possession is the love we are livin'.

Let's Make a Deal

I'll give up my hold on suffering, pain, and worry
if you'll replace it with love—and do it in a hurry.

I'll let go my grip on needing to be special
if in your arms I may once again nestle.

I'll release my grasp on worthlessness and guilt
if you will cause God's plan to be fulfilled.

What about it? Can't we make this deal?
Can't we bring the mind of God's one Son to heal?

Sweet Love's Glory

Oh, how I long to feel love's sweet caress,
to know its beauty, its tenderness,

to feel its warmth within my breast
as its soft lips upon mine are pressed.

Oh, tell me, dear Author, can't this be penned
within this tome, before its end?

Can't this sweet love in all its glory
be written into this life's story?

Meditation Writing XXXIII

I ask, "J, what would You say to me today?" His reply is as follows:

Greetings, My brother. You are one with the One, as am I. We are therefore truly one with each other. This is true of all persons. Our heritage is indeed holy. There is no one whom this is not true of. Leave no one aside. They are reflections of the Father, entitled to all His love. Why not practice extending His love to everyone? That is why you are here, to extend His love, that is, to express it, to push it out until it covers all of you. This is the nature of the Father, whose only desire is to see His love grow and grow. My love to you all. Please follow My lead. That is all.

Love,

J

Meditation Writing XXXIV

I ask, "J, what would You say to me today?" His reply is as follows:

Greetings, My brother. Keep on doing what you are doing. You will get nowhere if you let it go. You and all others are on the path back home to the Father. This is a place you have never left. The problem is that you believe that you have. Therefore, the answer is to awaken from this illusion of time and space. You cannot awaken while you continue to get caught up in the idea of separation. All is one! Remember this! Practice seeing it over and over and over! This belief in separation *must* be abandoned! When it is, you will awaken. Judgment is the lock on the door to heaven. Forgiveness is the key that opens it. Enter through the doorway now. Come in. I invite you and your friends to join me inside. There is love here. That is all.

Love,

J

My Big Brother

Ever since the loss of our mother,
no one cared for me more than my big brother.

He was always there when I needed assistance.
When asked for help, he offered no resistance.

He was strong for me when I felt weak,
when my own resources needed a tweak.

He shared with me his joy and his pain,
and he listened to me as I tried to explain

the joys and the sorrows of the life I'd led,
all the things I wish I'd said,

and all the things I'd left undone,
all the shortcomings of this younger one.

So now as he approaches his trip across the great sea,
I want him to know how much he's meant to me,

how much I'm grateful for his presence in my life
as I muddled through all the struggle and the strife.

Thank you, Pres, for being my big brother.
The role you played could be done by no other.
I love you.

The Busted Toy

When I was just a little boy,
you busted up my favorite toy.

But that was a long, long time ago,
and now's the time to just let it go.

I've forgiven you for what you did not do,
for I've come to understand this world isn't true.

Let go of all the guilt you feel,
because none of this is even real.

Let go of all the mistakes you've made,
and remember this world is a masquerade.

Let go of all your thoughts of fear,
and remember you're not even here.

Forgive yourself, forgive how you feel.
Forgive the world; it's not even real.

For you are asleep, the dreamer of the dream,
and none of this is what it may seem.

Ode to My Dad

I now take paper and pen to write this ode to my dad.
It's tough to remember the good times we had.

My recollections, as I now find,
are of the criticisms that filled my mind.

My judgments of him and all his rage,
would be more than enough to fill this page.

But I now see a boy who was filled with fear,
who never had anyone hold *him* near,

and let his tears stream down his face
as he let go of his fears, cleared out his space.

So now as I take this time to ponder and think,
I know that his pain pushed him to drink.

How can I blame him for what he did when he drank?
I walked the same road, and into the same hell I sank.

Ode to Myself

Seldom have I had the urge to let go of self-blame.
I've stubbornly held on to the guilt and the shame.

But now I give myself credit for the willingness to heal,
the willingness to experience all the love that I feel,

the willingness to forgive all my perceived wrongs,
the willingness to create new poems and new songs,

the willingness—no, the eagerness, I say—
to live a life of peace, for peace is the way.

So, I choose to let go of judgment and of pain.
I choose to let go of a world that is insane.

I choose to throw out the blocks to love's presence
and to live in the Truth, an expression of God's essence.

The Girl on the Butterfly Wing

The neurosurgeon, in all his glory,
could not accept a near-death story.

He, of doubtful mind,
needed proof, the scientific kind.

Then *he* contracted a rare disease
that literally drove him to his knees.

And the doctor, regardless of his diploma,
fell into a lengthy coma.

While there, he met a lovely young thing.
She was seated on a butterfly wing.

And oh, how she did beguile,
this beautiful young girl with her lovely smile.

She said, "I'll tell you this before I go.
There are three things that you must know:

You are loved and held to be so dear,
and there is nothing you ever need to fear.

There is no wrong that you can do.
All these things are really quite true.

Remember these." She uttered as she took her leave,
"For these three things you must believe."

When he came to in his hospital bed,
he did remember what the young girl said.

Later, he learned that he had a sister.
He never knew her, so he had not missed her.

She had passed away ten years before
and had arrived on heaven's shore.

Seeing her photo, his heart began to sing.
It was the lovely young girl on the butterfly wing.

Now he *sees proof* of heaven's existence.
And to near-death stories, he offers no resistance.

Celebrate

Weep not for me.
For I am more than you can see.

Do not sob and do not wail,
for I have broken out of jail.

I am on my way home at last,
free of guilt and free of the past,

free of this world and all its strife,
on my way home to eternal life.

I leave with you my love and gratitude,
for I now possess a brand-new attitude.

Love and acceptance are my new way.
In this world of the ego, I choose not to stay.

So, smile at me and wave your hand.
Celebrate! Strike up the band!

I'm more than you can see,
much more to understand.

Thoughts upon Awakening

Upon awakening, I found that the movie *Wizard of Oz* was running through my mind. I had the following interpretations of it:

Dorothy is a young girl who finds herself in an unfamiliar world, and her only desire is to return home.

When she asks for help with her problem, she is told by the people of Oz that the "wizard" is the only one who can help her.

They tell her that she needs to follow the yellow brick road. It was explained to me that the yellow bricks are like the gold ingots stored at Fort Knox. She is being told to follow the money. And all the people who are telling her this are spiritual midgets.

So, as she begins to follow the yellow brick road, she happens upon the Tin Man, someone who seems to be made of a hard metal substance, who can feel nothing and cannot cry.

It was asked of me if I had ever known anyone like that. I had to admit that I had, and I even had been that way myself from time to time.

They then come upon the Scarecrow, someone who thinks that if he only had a brain, he could figure everything out.

I was asked if I had ever known anyone like that, and I had to admit that I had—and that *I* have often been that way.

They then come upon the Cowardly Lion, someone who thinks that if only he were to roar loud enough, no one could see how fearful he really was.

When asked if I had ever known anyone like that, I again admitted that I had. My own father was that way. And then I reluctantly admitted that I sometimes had also been that way, even when I did not want to.

They then follow the yellow brick road all the way to the end.

I was asked if I had ever done that, and I again had to admit that I had and that it had solved *none* of my problems.

So, they finally come upon the "wizard," who is busy pulling strings, pushing buttons, pulling levers, and using smoke and mirrors to make the world of Oz *appear* to be real. When they pull back the curtain to expose the "wizard," they see an ordinary man who is pretending to be what he is not. And when Dorothy accuses him of being a fake and a bad man, he replies that he is not a bad man, he is just a bad wizard.

It was explained to me that the wizard is really the ego trying to convince me of the reality of the *unreal*! And he is using every trick, every ruse, all magic available, to help him do it.

After a few more attempts by the wizard to make the characters feel better about themselves, Dorothy finally *wakes up* to discover that the whole thing is actually a *dream*!

When asked who he *really* was, Buddha said, "I am someone who is waking up."

He also said, "Everything is unreal. Just like a dream."

Jesus said, "I am in this world, but I am not of it."

"Am I dreaming that I am dreaming?" —Chuang Tzu

"Am I Lao-tzu dreaming I am a butterfly, or am I a butterfly dreaming I am Lao-tzu?" —Lao-tzu, ancient teacher of the Tao (the Way), Chinese spiritual tradition.

"All the world's a stage, and all the men and women merely players. They have their exits and their entrances, and one man in his time plays many parts." —William Shakespeare

"Reality is merely an illusion, albeit a persistent one." —Albert Einstein

"Nothing real can be threatened. Nothing unreal exists." —*A Course in Miracles*

"Nothing leads you along more than illusion." —Faouzi Skali (Moroccan anthropologist)

In the book *Conversations with God*, author Neale Donald Walsch asks God how He could allow catastrophes and natural disasters to occur. God replies, "If your children are out playing and you *know* they're safe, do you care what games they are playing?"

Row, row, row your boat gently *down* the stream (not *up* the stream). Merrily, merrily, merrily, merrily, merrily (have fun and don't resist the stream), *life is but a dream!*